SOCIAL ANTHROPOLOGY

ANTHROPOLOGY AND ETHNOGRAPHY

Routledge Library Editions
Anthropology and Ethnography

SOCIAL AND CULTURAL ANTHROPOLOGY
In 16 Volumes

SOCIAL ANTHROPOLOGY

E E EVANS-PRITCHARD

Routledge
Taylor & Francis Group

LONDON AND NEW YORK

First published in 1951

Reprinted in 2004 by
Routledge
2 Park Square, Milton Park, Abingdon, Oxon, OX14 4RN
Simultaneously published in the USA and Canada by Routledge
711 Third Avenue, New York, NY 10017
Transferred to Digital Printing 2006
Routledge is an imprint of the Taylor & Francis Group
First issued in paperback 2013

The publishers have made every effort to contact authors/copyright
holders of the works reprinted in *Routledge Library Editions –
Anthropology and Ethnography*. This has not been possible in every case,
however, and we would welcome correspondence from those
individuals/companies we have been unable to trace.

These reprints are taken from original copies of each book. In many
cases the condition of these originals is not perfect. The publisher has
gone to great lengths to ensure the quality of these reprints, but wishes
to point out that certain characteristics of the original copies will, of
necessity, be apparent in reprints thereof.

British Library Cataloguing in Publication Data
A CIP catalogue record for this book is available from the British Library

Social Anthropology
ISBN 978-0-415-33030-5 (hbk)
ISBN 978-0-415-85070-4 (pbk)
Miniset: Social and Cultural Anthropology

Series: Routledge Library Editions – Anthropology and Ethnography

SOCIAL ANTHROPOLOGY

by

E. E. EVANS-PRITCHARD

Professor of Social Anthropology and Fellow of All Souls College, Oxford

ROUTLEDGE & KEGAN PAUL LTD

BROADWAY HOUSE, 68-74 CARTER LANE

LONDON, EC4V 5EL

First published 1951
Reprinted 1954, 1956, 1960, 1962, 1964, 1967, 1969 and 1972

ISBN 0 7100 1346 9 (c)
ISBN 0 7100 2893 8 (p)

PREFACE

These six lectures were given on the Third Programme of the B.B.C. in the winter of 1950. Except for a few minor verbal alterations they are printed as they were delivered. I thought it unwise to change, or add to, what·was written to be spoken within the limits imposed by the medium of expression and for a particular purpose and audience.

Social anthropology is still little more than a name to most people, and I hoped that broadcast talks on the subject would make its scope and methods better known. I trust that their publication as a book will serve the same purpose. As there are few brief introductory guides to social anthropology I believe that this book may also be of use to students in anthropological departments in British and American universities. I have therefore added a short bibliography.

I have expressed many of the ideas in these lectures before, and sometimes in the same language. I am grateful for permission to use them again to the Delegates of the Clarendon Press and to the Editors of *Man*, *Blackfriars*, and *Africa*.[1]

I thank Mr. K. O. L. Burridge for assistance in the preparation of the lectures and my colleagues at the Institute of Social Anthropology at Oxford and Mr. T. B. Radley of the B.B.C. for critical comments on them.

E. E. E-P.

[1] *Social Anthropology*, an Inaugural Lecture delivered before the University of Oxford on 4 February 1948, the Clarendon Press, 1948; 'Social Anthropology: Past and Present', the Marett Lecture, delivered in Exeter College Hall, Oxford, on 3 June 1950, *Man*, 1950, No. 198; 'Social Anthropology', *Blackfriars*, 1946; 'Applied Anthropology', a lecture given to the Oxford University Anthropological Society on 29 November 1945, *Africa*, 1946.

CONTENTS

I

THE SCOPE OF THE SUBJECT

I shall endeavour in these lectures to give you a general account of what social anthropology is. I am aware that even among well-read laymen there is a good deal of haziness about the subject. The words seem to arouse vague associations of either apes and skulls or strange rites of savages and curious superstitions. I do not think that I shall have any difficulty in convincing you that these associations are misplaced.

My treatment of the subject must be guided by this awareness. I must assume that some of you are frankly ignorant of what social anthropology is, and that others believe it to be what it is not. Those who have some acquaintance with the subject will, I hope, forgive me if, therefore, I discuss it broadly and in what may appear to them an elementary way.

In this, my first, lecture I shall tell you what is the general scope of the subject. In my second and third lectures I shall trace its theoretical development. In my fourth lecture I shall discuss that part of its research we call fieldwork. In my fifth lecture I shall illustrate the development of both theory and fieldwork by giving you some examples of modern studies. In my final lecture I shall discuss the relation of social anthropology to practical affairs.

I shall throughout restrict my account as far as possible to social anthropology in England, chiefly in order to avoid difficulties in presentation, for were I to give also an account of the development of the subject in continental countries and in America I should be compelled so to compress the material that what would be gained in comprehensiveness would not compensate for what would be lost in clarity and continuity. This restriction matters less than it would perhaps do in many other fields of learning because social anthropology has to a large extent developed independently in England. I shall, however, mention foreign writers and tendencies where these have markedly affected the thought of English scholars.

Even within these limits it is not easy to give you a clear and simple account of the aims and methods of social anthropology, because there is often lack of agreement about them among social anthropologists themselves. There is, of course, substantial agreement about many matters, but about others there are divergent opinions, and these, as often happens in a small and new subject, tend to become entangled with personalities, for scholars are perhaps more, rather than less, prone than other people to identify themselves with their opinions.

Personal preferences, when it is necessary to express them, are harmless if openly acknowledged. Ambiguities are more dangerous. Social anthropology has a very limited technical vocabulary, so that it has to use every-day language and this, as we all know, is not very precise. Such words as 'society', 'culture', 'custom', 'religion', 'sanction', 'structure', 'function', 'political', and 'democratic' do not always convey the same meaning either to different people or in different contexts. It would be possible for anthropologists to introduce many new words or to give a restricted and technical meaning to words in common use, but apart from the difficulty of getting their colleagues to agree to these usages, were this done on a large scale anthropological writings would soon become a jargon intelligible only to professional scholars. If we have to choose between steering close to the obscurities of everyday speech and the obscurities of specialist jargon I would prefer to risk the lesser perils of everyday speech, for what social anthropology has to teach concerns everybody and not only those who study it professionally.

Social anthropology is a title used in England and to some extent in the United States, to designate a department of the larger subject of anthropology, the study of man from a number of aspects. It concerns itself with human cultures and societies. On the continent a different terminology prevails. There when people speak of anthropology, which to us is the entire study of man, they have in mind only what we in England call physical anthropology, that is to say, the biological study of man. What we call social anthropology would be referred to on the continent as either ethnology or sociology.

Even in England the expression 'social anthropology' has only very recently come into use. The subject has been taught, under the names of anthropology or ethnology, since 1884 at Oxford, since 1900 at Cambridge, and since 1908 in London, but the first university chair which bore the title of *social anthropology* was the honorary professorship held by Sir James Frazer at Liverpool in 1908. The subject has recently received wider recognition and social anthropology is now taught under that name in a number of universities in Great Britain and in the Dominions.

Being a branch of the wider subject of anthropology, it is generally taught in connection with its other branches: physical anthropology, ethnology, prehistoric archaeology, and sometimes general linguistics and human geography. As the last two subjects seldom figure in degree and diploma courses in anthropology in this country I say no more about them; and all I need say about physical anthropology, since it has a very limited overlap with social anthropology at the present time, is that it is a branch of human biology and comprises such interests as heredity, nutrition, sex differences, the comparative anatomy and physiology of races, and the theory of human evolution.

It is with ethnology that we have our closest ties. To understand why this is so it is necessary to know that while social anthropologists consider that their subject embraces all human cultures and societies, including our own, they have, for reasons I will mention later, for the most part given their attention to those of primitive peoples. Ethnologists are dealing with the same peoples, and there is consequently a considerable overlap between the two subjects.

It is important to appreciate, however, that though ethnology and social anthropology make their studies very largely among the same range of peoples they make them with very different purposes. Consequently, though in the past no clear distinction was made between ethnology and social anthropology, they are today regarded as separate disciplines. The task of ethnology is to classify peoples on the basis of their racial and cultural characteristics and then to explain their distribution at the present time, or in past times, by the movement and mixture of peoples and the diffusion of cultures.

The classification of peoples and cultures is an essential preliminary to the comparisons which social anthropologists make between primitive societies, because it is highly convenient, and even necessary, to start by comparing those of the same general cultural type—those which belong to what Bastian long ago called 'geographical provinces'.[1]   When, however, ethnologists attempt to reconstruct the history of primitive peoples, for whose past historical records are lacking, they are compelled to rely on inferences from circumstantial

[1] Adolf Bastian, *Controversen in der Ethnologie*, 1893.

evidence to reach their conclusions, which, in the nature of the case, can never be more than probable reconstructions. Sometimes a number of different, and even contrary, hypotheses fit the facts equally well. Ethnology is thus not history in the ordinary sense, for history tells us not that events may have happened, but that they did happen, and not merely that events have taken place, but how and when they happened, and often why they happened. For this reason, and because ethnology can in any case tell us little about the past social life of primitive peoples, its speculations, as distinct from its classifications, have limited significance for social anthropologists.

Prehistoric archaeology is best regarded as a branch of ethnology. It attempts to reconstruct the history of peoples and cultures from human and cultural remains found by excavation in geological deposits. It also relies on circumstantial evidence and, like ethnology, can tell social anthropologists little about the ideas and institutions, in which they would be interested, of the peoples whose bones and artifacts it discovers and classifies. Another branch of anthropology, comparative technology, in the main the comparative technology of primitive peoples, is, as it is usually taught, an adjunct of ethnology and prehistory.

Social anthropology has quite a different task to perform. It studies, as I shall soon demonstrate, social behaviour, generally in institutionalized forms, such as the family, kinship systems, political organization, legal procedures, religious cults, and the like, and the relations between such institutions; and it studies them either in contemporaneous societies or in historical societies for which there is adequate information of the kind to make such studies feasible.

So, whereas some custom of a people, when plotted on a distribution map, is of interest for the ethnologist as evidence of an ethnic movement, of a cultural drift, or of past contact between peoples, it is of interest to the social anthropologist as part of the whole social life of the people at the present time. The mere probability that they may have borrowed it from some other people is not very significant for him since he cannot know for certain that they did borrow it and, even if they did, he does not know when, how, and why they borrowed it. For example, certain peoples in East Africa take the sun for their symbol of God. This to some ethnologists is evidence of Ancient Egyptian influence. The social anthropologist, knowing that it cannot be proved whether this hypothesis is right or wrong, is more concerned to relate the solar symbolism to the whole systems of belief and cult of these peoples. Thus, while the ethnologist and the social anthropologist may make use of the same ethnographic data, they use them for different purposes.

The curricula of university courses in anthropology may be figured by three intersecting circles representing biological studies, historical studies, and sociological studies, the overlapping sections of which are physical anthropology, ethnology (including prehistoric archaeology and comparative technology), and social anthropology. Although these three anthropological disciplines have a common field in primitive man they have, as we have seen, very different aims and methods, and it is through historical circumstances, largely connected with the Darwinian theory of evolution, rather than as a result of a carefully thought out plan, that they are taught together in varying degrees in the universities and are jointly represented in the Royal Anthropological Institute.

Some of my colleagues have indeed expressed themselves dissatisfied with the present arrangement. Some of us would prefer to see social anthropology brought into a closer teaching relationship with psychology or with the so-called social sciences, such as general sociology, economics, and comparative politics, and others of us with other subjects. The question is complex, and this is not the occasion to discuss it. I will only say that the answer given to it much depends on the view taken of the nature of social anthropology, for there is a broad division of opinion between those who regard social anthropology as a natural science and those, like myself, who regard it as one of the humanities. This division is perhaps at its sharpest when relations between anthropology and history are being discussed. I shall leave consideration of this issue till a later lecture, because it is necessary to know something about the early development of the subject to perceive how the division of opinion has come about.

I have briefly, and in an inevitably discursive manner, outlined the position of social anthropology as a university subject. Having cleared the ground to some extent by so doing, I can now devote myself wholly to social anthropology, for that is the topic I am here to discuss and the only one I am competent to discuss. When therefore for convenience I speak in future of anthropology without the qualification 'social' it must be understood that it is to social anthropology that I refer.

I had better deal right away with the questions 'What are primitive societies?' and 'Why do we study them?' before telling you more precisely what we study in them. The word 'primitive' in the sense in which it has become established in anthropological literature does not mean that the societies it qualifies are either earlier in time or inferior to other kinds of societies. As far as we know, primitive societies have just as long a history as our own, and while they are less developed than our society in some respects they are often more developed in others. This being so, the word was perhaps an unfortunate choice, but it has now been too widely accepted as a technical term to be avoided.

SOCIAL ANTHROPOLOGY

It suffices to say at this stage that when anthropologists use it they do so in reference to those societies which are small in scale with regard to numbers, territory, and range of social contacts, and which have by comparison with more advanced societies a simple technology and economy and little specialization of social function. Some anthropologists would add further criteria, particularly the absence of literature, and hence of any systematic art, science, or theology.[1]

We are sometimes criticized for giving so much of our time to the study of these primitive societies. It is suggested that inquiry into problems of our own society might be more useful. This may be so, but for various reasons primitive societies have long held the attention of those interested in the study of social institutions. They attracted the notice of philosophers in the eighteenth century chiefly because they furnished examples of what was supposed to be man living in a state of nature before the institution of civil government. They engaged the attention of anthropologists in the nineteenth century because it was believed that they provided important clues in the search for the origins of institutions. Later anthropologists were interested in them because it was held that they displayed institutions in their simplest forms, and that it is sound method to proceed from examination of the more simple to examination of the more complex, in which what has been learnt from a study of the more simple would be an aid.

This last reason for interest in primitive societies gained in weight as the so-called functional anthropology of today developed, for the more it is regarded as the task of social anthropology to study social institutions as interdependent parts of social systems, the more it is seen to be an advantage to be able to study those societies which are

[1] Robert Redfield, 'The Folk Society', *The American Journal of Sociology*, 1947.

structurally so simple, and culturally so homogeneous, that they can be directly observed as wholes, before attempting to study complex civilized societies where this is not possible. Moreover, it is a matter of experience that it is easier to make observations among peoples with cultures unlike our own, the otherness in their way of life at once engaging attention, and that it is more likely that interpretations will be objective.

Another, and very cogent, reason for studying primitive societies at the present time is that they are rapidly being transformed and must be studied soon or never. These vanishing social systems are unique structural variations, a study of which aids us very considerably in understanding the nature of human society, because in a comparative study of institutions the number of societies studied is less significant than their range of variation. Quite apart from that consideration, the study of primitive societies has intrinsic value. They are interesting in themselves in that they provide descriptions of the way of life, the values, and the beliefs of peoples living without what we have come to regard as the minimum requirements of comfort and civilization.

We therefore feel it an obligation to make a systematic study of as many of these primitive societies as we can while there is still an opportunity to do so. There are a vast number of primitive societies and very few indeed have yet been studied intensively by anthropologists, for such studies take a long time and anthropologists are a very small body.

But though we give chief attention to primitive societies I must make it clear that we do not restrict our attention to them. In America, where social anthropology is better represented in the universities than in the British Empire, a number of important studies of more advanced societies have already been made by American or American-trained anthropologists—in Ireland, in Japan, in China, in India, in Mexico, in Canada, and in the United States itself. I shall give you in a later lecture some account of one of these studies, that by Arensberg and Kimball in Southern Ireland.

For various reasons, among them shortage of personnel and the great number of primitive peoples in our colonial empire, British anthropologists have lagged behind in this matter, but they also are broadening their studies to include peoples who cannot in any sense be described as primitive. During the past few years students of the Institute of Social Anthropology at Oxford have been engaged in studies of rural communities in India, the West Indies, Turkey, and Spain, of the Bedouin Arabs of North Africa, and of English village and urban life.

Also, though not to the same extent in recent years, studies have been made by anthropologists, or from an anthropological point of view, in historic societies, literary sources here taking the place of direct observation. I am thinking of such writings as those of Sir James Frazer on the ancient Hebrews and on certain aspects of Roman culture, of Sir William Ridgeway and Jane Harrison on Hellenic subjects, of Robertson Smith on early Arabian society, and of Hubert on the history of the Celts.

I must emphasize that, theoretically at any rate, social anthropology is the study of all human societies and not merely of primitive societies, even if in practice, and for convenience, at the present time its attention is mostly given to the institutions of the simpler peoples, for it is evident that there can be no separate discipline which restricts itself entirely to these societies. Though an anthropologist may be carrying out research among a primitive people, what he is studying among them are language, law, religion, political institutions, economics, and so forth, and he is therefore concerned with the same general problems as the student of these subjects in the great civilizations of the world. It must be remembered also that in interpreting his observations on primitive societies the anthropologist is always, if only implicitly, comparing them with his own.

Social anthropology can therefore be regarded as a branch of sociological studies, that branch which chiefly devotes itself to primitive societies. When people speak of sociology they generally have in mind studies of particular problems in civilized societies. If we give this sense to the word, then the difference between social anthropology and sociology is a difference of field, but there are also important differences of method between them. The social anthropologist studies primitive societies directly, living among them for months or years, whereas socio-logical research is usually from documents and largely statistical. The social anthropologist studies societies as wholes. He studies their oecologies, their economics, their legal and political institutions, their family and kin-ship organizations, their religions, their technologies, their arts, *etc.* as parts of general social systems. The sociologist's work, on the other hand, is usually very specialized, being a study of isolated problems, such as divorce, crime, insanity, labour unrest, and incentives in industry. Sociology is very largely mixed with social philosophy at one end and social planning at the other. It seeks not only to discover how institutions work but to decide how they ought to work and to alter them, while social anthropology has mostly kept apart from such considerations.

However, it is not in this sense that I speak of sociology in these lectures, but in the broader sense in which it is regarded as a general body of theoretical knowledge about human societies. It is the relation of this general body of theory to primitive social life which constitutes the subject of social anthropology. This will be evident when I give you some account of its history because much of our theoretical, or conceptual, knowledge is derived from writings which are in no way, or only indirectly, concerned with primitive societies at all. Therefore I will ask you to keep in mind throughout these lectures two interconnected developments, the growth of sociological theory, of which anthropological theory is only a part, and the growth of knowledge about primitive societies to which sociological theory has been submitted and re-formulated as a specialized body of knowledge relating to them.

I must now give you, in the light of this discussion about the place of social anthropology as a department in a wider field of learning, a clearer idea of the kind of problems social anthropologists investigate. A good way of doing this is to tell you some of the subjects about which post-graduate students of anthropology at Oxford have written theses during the last few years.

I give you the titles of a few which have been awarded degrees recently: 'The position of the chief in the modern political system of Ashanti (West Africa), A study of the influence of contemporary social changes on Ashanti institutions.'; 'The social function of religion in a South Indian community' (the Coorgs); 'The political organization of the Nandi' (East Africa); 'The social structure of Jamaica, with special reference to racial distinctions'; 'The function of bridewealth in selected African societies'; 'A study of the symbolism of political authority in Africa'; 'A comparative study of the forms of slavery'; 'The social organization of the Yao of southern Nyasaland' (Central Africa); 'Systems of land tenure among the Bantu peoples of East Africa'; 'The status of women among the southern Bantu' (South Africa); 'An investigation into the social sanctions of the Naga tribes of the Indo-Burma border'; 'The political system of the Murle' (East Africa); 'The political organization of the Plains Indians' (North America); 'A study of inter-state boundary litigation in

Ashanti' (West Africa); 'Aspects of rank in Melanesia'; 'The social organization of the central and eastern Eskimo'; 'Delict in primitive law' (Indonesia and Africa).

You will, I hope, gain from this sample a general impression of the kind of work social anthropologists do. You will note in the first place that there is nothing very exciting about the subjects of these theses, no seeking after the strange or colourful, no appeal to antiquarian or romantic interests. All are matter-of-fact inquiries into one or other type of social institution.

You will observe also that in so far as the theses discuss particular peoples or series of peoples, they are distributed over all parts of Africa, Southern India, Jamaica, the Indo-Burma frontier, North America, the Polar Regions, islands of the Pacific, and Indonesia. I draw attention to this geographical spread because the vastness of the anthropological field, while offering opportunities for research for the most diverse interests, involves, as I will explain later, certain difficulties in teaching and, to an increasing extent, regional specialization. In the narrowest interpretation of its province it includes the Polynesian and Melanesian peoples of the Pacific, the aboriginals of Australia, the Lapp and Eskimo peoples of the Polar regions, the Mongolian peoples of Siberia, the Negro peoples of Africa, the Indian peoples of the American continent, and the more backward peoples of India, Burma, Malay, and Indonesia—many thousands of different cultures and societies. On a wider interpretation its boundaries include also the more advanced, but still relatively simple, peoples of near and further Asia, north Africa, and parts of Europe—an almost limitless number of cultures and sub-cultures and societies and sub-societies.

You will also note that the sample includes studies of political institutions, religious institutions, class distinctions based on colour, sex, or rank, economic institutions, legal or quasi-legal institutions, and marriage, and also of social adaptation, and of the entire social organization, or structure, of one or other people. Social anthropology thus not only covers societies round the globe but also a number of different studies. Indeed, any adequately staffed department of anthropology tries to cover in its courses of lectures on primitive societies at least the minimum and essential topics of kinship and the family, comparative political institutions, comparative economics, comparative religion, and comparative law, as well as more general courses on the study of institutions, general sociological theory, and the history of social anthropology. It gives also special courses on the societies of selected ethno-geographical regions; and it may provide courses besides on such particular subjects as morals, magic, mythology, primitive science, primitive art, primitive technology, and language, and also on the writings of particular anthropologists and sociologists.

It stands to reason that though an anthropologist may have a general knowledge of all these different ethnographic regions and sociological disciplines, he can be an authority in only one or two of each. Consequently, as in all fields of learning, as knowledge increases there takes place specialization. The anthropologist becomes a specialist in African studies, in Melanesian studies, in American Indian studies, and so forth. He then no longer attempts to master the detail of regions other than those of his choice, except in so far as it is embodied in monographs explicitly devoted to general problems, perhaps religious or legal institutions, in which he is particularly interested. There is already a sufficiently abundant literature on, for example, the American Indians or the African Bantu for a scholar to devote himself exclusively to the one or the other.

The tendency towards specialization becomes yet more marked when the peoples concerned have a literature or belong to a wider culture with a literary tradition. If one has any regard for scholarship one cannot be a student of Arab Bedouin or peasants without a knowledge not only of their spoken language but also of the classical language of their cultural hinterland, or of Indian peasant communities without having some knowledge both of the literature of their language and of Sanskrit, the classical language of their ritual and religious tradition. Also, the anthropologist, besides restricting his researches to certain regions has to devote himself primarily to one or two topics if he is to be master of them and not a jack of all trades. One cannot adequately make a comparative study of primitive legal systems without a good background of general law and jurisprudence, or of primitive art without being well-read in the literature of art.

The circumstances I have related make social anthropology difficult to teach, especially when, as for the most part at Oxford, it is taught at the post-graduate and research level. When a large number of students are working on material in widely separated parts of the world and on a wide variety of problems it is often impossible to give them more than very general supervision. Sir Charles Oman tells us that the same situation confronted those Regius Professors of History at Oxford who tried, unsuccessfully, to conduct classes for post-graduates, for, as he wistfully remarks, 'post-graduate students wander at their own sweet will'.[1] However, the situation is not so difficult in social anthropology as it is in history, for social anthropology is more able to generalize and has a body of general theory which history lacks. There are not only many overt similarities between primitive societies all over the world but they can, at any rate to some extent, be classified by structural analysis into a limited number of types. This gives a unity to the subject. Social anthropologists study a primitive society in the same way

[1] Sir Charles Oman, *On the Writing of History*, 1939, p. 252.

whether it is in Polynesia, Africa, or Lapland; and whatever they are writing about—a kinship system, a religious cult, or a political institution—it is examined in its relation to the total social structure in which it is contained.

Before considering, even in a preliminary manner, what we understand by social structure I will ask you to note a further characteristic of these theses, because it brings out a significant problem in anthropology at the present time and one which I shall discuss again in later lectures. They are all written on sociological themes, that is to say, they deal fundamentally with sets of social relations, relations between members of a society and between social groups. The point I want to make here is that they are studies of societies rather than of cultures. There is an extremely important difference between the two concepts which has led anthropological research and theory in two different directions.

Allow me to give a few simple examples. If you go into an English church you will see that men remove their head-dress but keep their shoes on, but if you enter a mosque in a Muslim land you will observe that men remove their shoes but keep their head-dress on. The same behaviour is customary when entering an English house or a Bedouin tent. These are differences of culture or custom. The purpose and function of the behaviour is the same in both cases, to show respect, but it is expressed differently in the two cultures. Let me give you a more complex example. Nomadic Bedouin Arabs have in some, and basic, respects the same kind of social structure as some of the semi-nomadic Nilotic peoples of East Africa, but culturally the two peoples are different. Bedouin live in tents, Nilotics in huts and windscreens; Bedouin herd camels, Nilotics cattle; Bedouin are Muslims, Nilotics have a different kind of religion; and so forth. A different sort of example, and an even more complex one, would be the distinction we make when we speak of Hellenic or Hindu civilization and Hellenic or Hindu society.

We are here dealing with two different concepts, or two different abstractions from the same reality. Though the definitions which should be given to each and their relation to one another have often been discussed, they have seldom been systematically examined, and there is still much confusion and little unanimity about the matter. Among the older anthropological writers, Morgan, Spencer, and Durkheim conceived the aim of what we now call social anthropology to be the classification and functional analysis of social structures. This point of view has persisted among Durkheim's followers in France. It is also well represented in British anthropology today and in the tradition of formal sociology in Germany.[1] Tylor on the other hand, and others who leant towards ethnology, conceived its aim to be the classification and analysis of cultures, and this has been the dominant viewpoint in American anthropology for a long time, partly, I think, because the fractionized and disintegrated Indian societies on which their research has been concentrated lend themselves more easily to studies of culture than of social structure; partly because the absence of a tradition of intensive fieldwork through the native languages and for long periods of time, such as we have in England, also tends towards studies of custom or culture rather than of social relations; and partly for other reasons.

When a social anthropologist describes a primitive society the distinction between society and culture is obscured by the fact that he describes the reality, the raw behaviour, in which both are contained. He tells you, for example, the precise manner in which a man

[1] Georg Simmel, *Soziologie*, 1908; Leopold von Wiese, *Allgemeine Soziologie*, 1924.

shows respect to his ancestors; but when he comes to interpret the behaviour he has to make abstractions from it in the light of the particular problems he is investigating. If these are problems of social structure he pays attention to the social relationships of the persons concerned in the whole procedure rather than to the details of its cultural expression.

Thus one, or a partial, interpretation of ancestor worship might be to show how it is consistent with family or kinship structure. The cultural, or customary, actions which a man performs when showing respect to his ancestors, the facts, for instance, that he makes a sacrifice and that what he sacrifices is a cow or an ox, require a different kind of interpretation, and this may be partly both psychological and historical.

This methodological distinction is most evident when comparative studies are undertaken, for to attempt both kinds of interpretation at the same time is then almost certain to lead to confusion. In comparative studies what one compares are not things in themselves but certain particular characteristics of them. If one wishes to make a sociological comparison of ancestor cults in a number of different societies, what one compares are sets of structural relations between persons. One necessarily starts, therefore, by abstracting these relations in each society from their particular modes of cultural expression. Otherwise one will not be able to make the comparison. What one is doing is to set apart problems of a certain kind for purposes of research. In doing this, one is not making a distinction between different kinds of thing—society and culture are not entities—but between different kinds of abstraction.

I have spoken earlier of social anthropology's studying the cultures and societies of primitive peoples, because I did not want at that stage to introduce this difficulty. I have stated it, and I shall have to leave the matter there, only asking you to bear in mind that there is still uncertainty and division of opinion about it and that it is a very difficult and complex problem. I shall only say further that the study of problems of culture leads, and I think must lead, to the framing of them in terms of history or psychology, whereas problems of society are framed in terms of sociology. My own view is that while both kinds of problems are equally important, structural studies ought to be made first.

This brings me back to the theses once again. Had you read them you would have noted that they have this in common, that they examine whatever it is they set out to examine—chieftainship, religion, race distinctions, bride-wealth, slavery, land tenure, the status of women, social sanctions, rank, legal procedures, or whatever it may be —not as isolated and self-contained institutions but as parts of social structures and in terms of these structures. What then is a social structure? I shall have to be rather vague and inconclusive in answering this question in my introductory lecture. I shall discuss it again in later lectures, but I may as well say right away that, here again, there is much divergence of opinion on the matter. This is inevitable. Such basic concepts cannot be given precise definition. However, if we are to proceed further, I must give you at any rate a preliminary indication of what is generally implied by the term structure.

It is evident that there must be uniformities and regularities in social life, that a society must have some sort of order, or its members could not live together. It is only because people know the kind of behaviour expected of them, and what kind of behaviour to expect from others, in the various situations of social life, and co-ordinate their activities in submission to rules and under the guidance of values that each and all are able to go about their affairs. They can make predictions, antici-pate events, and lead their lives in harmony with their fellows because every society has a form or pattern which allows us to speak of it as a system, or structure, within which, and in accordance with which, its members live their lives. The use of the word structure in this sense implies that there is some kind of consistency between its parts, at any rate up to the point of open contradiction and conflict being avoided, and that it has greater durability than most of the fleeting things of human life. The people who live in any society may be unaware, or only dimly aware, that it has a structure. It is the task of the social anthropologist to reveal it.

A total social structure, that is to say the entire structure of a given society, is composed of a number of subsidiary structures or systems, and we may speak of its kinship system, its economic system, its religious system and its political system.

The social activities within these systems or structures are organized round institutions such as marriage, the family, markets, chieftainship, and so forth; and when we speak of the functions of these institutions we mean the part they play in the maintenance of the structure.

I think that all social anthropologists would accept, more or less, these definitions. It is when we begin to ask what kind of abstraction a social structure is and what precisely is meant by the functioning of an institution that we meet with difficulties and divergence of opinion. The issues will, I think, be better understood after I have given some account of the theoretical development of social anthropology.

II

THEORETICAL BEGINNINGS

In this, my second, lecture and in the following lecture I propose to give you some account of the history of social anthropology. I do not intend to present you with a mere chronological arrangement of anthropologists and their books, but to attempt to trace the development of its general concepts, or theory, using some of these writers and their works as illustrations of this development.[1]

As we have seen, social anthropology is a very new subject in the sense that it has only recently been taught in our universities, and still more recently under that title. In another sense it may be said to have begun with the earliest speculations of mankind, for everywhere and at all times men have propounded theories about the nature of society. In this sense there is no definite point at which social anthropology can be said to have begun. Nevertheless, there is a point beyond which it is hardly profitable to trace back its development. This nascent period of our subject was the eighteenth century. It is a child of the Enlightenment and bears throughout its history and today many of the characteristic features of its ancestry.

In France its lineage runs from Montesquieu (1689–1755). His best known book, *De L'Esprit des Lois* (1748),

[1] General accounts of the history of anthropology can be found in A. C. Haddon, *History of Anthropology*, revised edit., 1934; Paul Radin, *The Method and Theory of Ethnology*, 1933; T. K. Penniman, *A Hundred Years of Anthropology*, 1935; and Robert H. Lowie, *The History of Ethnological Theory*, 1937.

a treatise on political, or perhaps social, philosophy, is best remembered for some rather odd notions Montesquieu had about the influence of climate on the character of peoples and for his remarks on the separation of powers in government. But what is of chief interest to us is that he had the idea of everything in a society and its ambient being functionally related to everything else. One can only understand international, constitutional, criminal, and civil law by considering them in relation to each other and also in relation to the physical environment of a people, their economy, their numbers, their beliefs, their customs and manners, and their temperaments. The object of his book is to examine 'all these interrelations: they form taken together that which one calls the Spirit of the Laws'.[1]

Montesquieu used the word 'laws' in a number of different senses, but in a general sense he meant 'the necessary relations which derive from the nature of things',[2] that is to say, the conditions which make human society possible at all and those conditions which make any particular type of society possible. Time will not allow me to discuss his argument in detail, but it should, I think, be noted that he distinguished between the 'nature' of society and its 'principle', its 'nature' being 'that which makes it to be what it is' and its 'principle' being 'that which makes it function'. 'The one is its particular structure, and the other the human passions which make it work'.[3] He thus distinguished between a social structure and the system of values which operate in it.

From Montesquieu the French lineage of social anthropology runs through such writers as D'Alembert, Condorcet, Turgot, and in general the Encyclopaedists and

[1] *De L'Esprit des Lois*, edited by Gonzague Truc, Editions Garnier Frères, n.d., p. 11.
[2] Ibid., p. 5.   [3] Ibid., p. 23.

22

Physiocrats, to Saint Simon (1760–1825), who was the first to propose clearly a science of society. This descendant of an illustrious family was a very remarkable person. A true child of the Enlightenment, he believed passionately in science and progress and desired above all to establish a positive science of social relations, which were to him analogous to the organic relations of physiology; and he insisted that scientists must analyse facts and not concepts. It is understandable that his disciples were socialists and collectivists, and perhaps also that the movement ended in religious fervour and finally evaporated in a search for the perfect woman who would play the part of a female messiah. Saint Simon's best known disciple, who later quarrelled with him, was Auguste Comte (1798–1857). Comte, a more systematic thinker than Saint Simon, though just as eccentric a person, named the proposed new science of society 'sociology'. The stream of French philosophical rationalism which comes from these writers was later, through the writings of Durkheim and his students and Lévy-Bruhl, who were in the direct line of Saint Simonian tradition, to colour English anthropology strongly.

Our forbears in Great Britain were the Scottish moral philosophers, whose writings were typical of the eighteenth century. The best known names are David Hume (1711–1776) and Adam Smith (1723–1790). Most of them are very little read today. They insisted that societies are natural systems. By this they meant in particular that society derives from human nature and not from a social contract, about which Hobbes and others had written so much. It was in this sense that they talked about natural morality, natural religion, natural jurisprudence, and so forth.

Being regarded as natural systems or organisms, societies must be studied empirically and inductively, and not by the methods of Cartesian rationalism. Thus, the title of Hume's thesis of 1739 was *A Treatise of Human Nature: Being an Attempt to introduce the experimental Method of Reasoning into Moral Subjects.* But they were also highly theoretical thinkers and were chiefly interested in the formulation of what they called general principles and what would today be called sociological laws.[1]

These philosophers had also a firm belief in limitless progress—what they called improvement and perfectibility—and in laws of progress. To discover these laws they made use of what Comte was later to call the comparative method. As they used it, it implied that, human nature being fundamentally everywhere and at all times the same, all peoples travel along the same road, and by uniform stages, in their gradual but continuous advance to perfection; though some more slowly than others.

It is true that there is no certain evidence of the earliest stages of our history but, human nature being constant, it may be assumed that our forefathers must have lived the same kind of life as the Redskins of America and other primitive peoples when they lived in similar conditions and at a similar level of culture. By comparing all known societies and arranging them in order of improvement it is thus possible to reconstruct what the history of our own society, and of all human societies, must have been, even though it cannot be known when or by what events progress took place.

Dugald Stewart called this procedure theoretical, or conjectural, history. It is a kind of philosophy of history which attempts to isolate broad general trends and tendencies and regards particular events as mere incidents. Its method is admirably set forth by Lord Kames: 'We must be satisfied with collecting the facts and circumstances as they may be gathered from the laws of different countries: and if these put together make a regular system of causes and effects, we may rationally

[1] Gladys Bryson, *Man and Society*, 1945, passim.

conclude, that the progress has been the same among all nations, in the capital circumstances at least; for accidents, or the singular nature of a people, or of a government, will always produce some peculiarities.'[1]

Since there are these laws of development and there is a method by which they can be discovered it follows that the science of man these philosophers proposed to establish is a normative science, aiming at the creation of a secularist ethics based on a study of human nature in society.

We have already in the speculations of these eighteenth-century writers all the ingredients of anthropological theory in the following century, and even at the present day: the emphasis on institutions, the assumption that human societies are natural systems, the insistence that the study of them must be empirical and inductive, that its purpose is the discovery and formulation of universal principles or laws, particularly in terms of stages of development revealed by the use of the comparative method of conjectural history, and that its ultimate purpose is the scientific determination of ethics.

It is on account of their attachment to the formulation of general principles and because they dealt with societies and not with individuals that these writers are of particular interest in the history of anthropology. In seeking to establish principles their concern was with institutions, their structural interrelations, their growth, and the human needs they arose to satisfy. Adam Ferguson, for example, in his *An Essay on the History of Civil Society* (1767) and other works writes of such matters as the manner of subsistence, varieties of the human race, the disposition of men to society, the principles of population growth, arts and commercial arrangements, and ranks and social divisions.

The importance of primitive societies for the questions which interested these philosophers is evident, and they

---

[1] Lord Kames, *Historical Law-Tracts*, vol. i, 1758, p. 37.

occasionally made use of what was known of them, but, outside their own culture and time, Old Testament and classical writings were their main sources. Little was, in any case, as yet known about primitive societies, though the voyages of discovery in the sixteenth century had even in Shakespeare's time led to a general representation of the savage in educated circles, portrayed in the character of Caliban; and writers on politics, law and custom were already beginning to be aware by that time of the great diversity of custom presented by peoples outside Europe. Montaigne (1533–1592), in particular, devoted many pages of his Essays to what we would today call ethnographic material.

In the seventeenth and eighteenth centuries philosophers cited primitive societies in support of their arguments about the nature of rude society in contrast to civil society, that is to say, society before the establishment of government by contract or acceptance of despotism. Locke (1632–1714) especially, refers to these societies in his speculations about religion, government and property. He was familiar with what had been written about the hunting Redskins of New England, and the fact that his knowledge was restricted to only one type of American Indian society much biassed his account.

French writers of the time drew their picture of man in a state of nature from what had been published about the Indians of the St. Lawrence, especially Gabriel Sagard's and Joseph Lafitau's accounts of the Hurons and Iroquois.[1] Rousseau's portrait of natural man was largely drawn from what was known of the Caribs of South America.

[1] Gabriel Sagard, *Le Grand Voyage du Pays des Hurons*, 1632; Joseph François Lafitau, *Moeurs des Sauvages Ameriquains comparées aux Moeurs des Premiers Temps*, 1724. For a general discussion of the influence of ethnographical writings on political philosophy see J. L. Myres, Presidential Address to Section H., *British Association for the Advancement of Science*, Winnipeg, 1909.

I have mentioned the use made of accounts of primitive peoples by some writers of the seventeenth and eighteenth centuries, because we can see in it the beginnings of that interest in the simpler societies as valuable material for theories about the nature and improvement of social institutions which in the middle of the nineteenth century was to develop into what we now call social anthropology.

The writers I have named, both in France and England, were of course in the sense of their time philosophers, and so regarded themselves. In spite of all their talk about empiricism they relied more on introspection and *a priori* reasoning than on observation of actual societies. For the most part—Montesquieu should perhaps be excepted from this stricture—they used facts to illustrate or corroborate theories reached by speculation. It was not till the middle of the nineteenth century that systematic studies of social institutions were made. In the decade between 1861 and 1871 there appeared books which we regard as our early theoretical classics: Maine's *Ancient Law* (1861) and his *Village-Communities in the East and West* (1871), Bachofen's *Das Mutterrecht* (1861), Fustel de Coulanges' *La Cité Antique* (1864), McLennan's *Primitive Marriage* (1865), Tylor's *Researches into the Early History of Mankind* (1865) and his *Primitive Culture* (1871), and Morgan's *Systems of Consanguinity and Affinity of the Human Family* (1871).

Not all these books were concerned primarily with primitive societies. Maine wrote about the early institutions of Rome and, more generally, of the Indo-European peoples, and Bachofen was chiefly interested in the traditions and mythologies of classical antiquity; but those which were least concerned with them dealt with comparable institutions at early periods in the development of historical societies and they dealt with them, as I shall show, in a sociological manner.

27

It was McLennan and Tylor in this country, and Morgan in America, who first treated primitive societies as a subject which might in itself engage the attention of serious scholars. It was they who first brought together the information about primitive peoples from a wide range of miscellaneous writings and presented it in systematic form, thereby laying the foundations of social anthropology. In their writings the study of primitive societies and speculative theory about the nature of social institutions met.

These authors of the middle of the nineteenth century, like the philosophers before them, were anxious to rid the study of social institutions of mere speculation. They, also, thought that they could do this by being strictly empirical and by rigorous use of the comparative method. We have noted that this method was utilized, under the title of hypothetical or conjectural history, by the moral philosophers. It was given a new and more precise definition by Comte in his *Cours de Philosophie Positive* (1830). As we shall see, it was later to be restated without its historicism by modern anthropology as the functional method.

According to Comte, there is a functional relation between social facts of different kinds, what Saint Simon and he called series of social facts, political, economic, religious, moral, *etc.* Changes in any one of these series provoke corresponding changes in the others. The establishment of these correspondences or interdependencies between one kind of social fact and another is the aim of sociology. It is attained by the logical method of concomitant variations, since in dealing with very complex social phenomena, in which simple variables cannot be isolated, this is the only method which can be pursued.

Using this method, not only the writers to whom I have referred, but also those who came after them, wrote many large volumes purporting to show the laws of the origin and development of social institutions: the development of monogamous marriage from promiscuity, of property from communism, of contract from status, of industry from nomadism, of positive science from theology, of monotheism from animism. Sometimes, especially when treating religion, explanations were sought in terms of psychological origins, what the philosophers had called human nature, as well as in terms of historical origins.

The two favourite topics for discussion were the development of the family and the development of religion. Victorian anthropologists were never tired of writing about these two subjects, and a consideration of some of their conclusions about them will help us to understand the general tone of anthropology at that time, for though they disputed violently among themselves about what could be inferred from the evidence, they were agreed about the aims and methods to be pursued.

Sir Henry Maine (1822–1888), a Scot, a lawyer, and the founder, in England, of comparative jurisprudence, held that the patriarchal family is the original and universal form of social life and that the *patria potestas*, the absolute authority of the patriarch, on which it rests has produced everywhere at a certain stage agnation, the tracing of descent through males exclusively. Another jurist, the Swiss Bachofen, reached a precisely opposite conclusion about the form of the primitive family; and it is curious that he and Maine published their conclusions in the same year. According to Bachofen, there was first everywhere promiscuity, then a matrilineal and matriarchal social system, and only late in the history of man did this system give way to a patrilineal and patriarchal one.

A third lawyer and another Scot, J. F. McLennan (1827–1881), was a great believer in general laws of social development, though he had his own paradigm of stages and ridiculed those of his contemporaries. In his view, early man must be assumed to have been promiscuous, though the evidence shows him first as living everywhere in small matrilineal and totemic stock-groups which practised the blood feud. These hordes were politically independent of one another and each was an exogamous group on account of the custom of female infanticide, which made it necessary for its menfolk to obtain wives from other tribal groups. These early societies eventually developed, by way of polyandry, a patrilineal, in the place of a matrilineal, system of descent, while the family slowly emerged in the form to which we are accustomed. First comes the tribe, then the gens or house, and lastly the family. McLennan's thesis was taken over by yet another Scot, the Old Testament scholar and one of the founders of comparative religion, William Robertson Smith (1846–1894), who applied it to the early records of Arab and Hebrew history.[1]

That versatile man Sir John Lubbock (1834–1913), later Baron Avebury, also traced the development of modern marriage from a state of pristine promiscuity[2]—it was an obsession of writers of the period. The most complicated, and in some respects the most fantastic, product of the comparative method was the construction of the American lawyer L. H. Morgan (1818–1881), who postulated, among other things, no less than fifteen stages of the development of marriage and the family, beginning with promiscuity and ending with monogamous marriage and the family of western civilization. This fanciful scheme of progress has been incorporated, through Engels, into the official Marxist doctrines of communist Russia.

In their reconstructions, these writers made much of the idea of what McLennan called 'symbols' and Tylor called 'survivals'. Social survivals were compared to the rudimentary organs found in some animals and to mute

---

[1] *Kinship and Marriage in Early Arabia*, 1885.
[2] *The Origin of Civilization*, 1870.

letters in words. They are functionless, or at any rate, if they have a function, it is secondary and different to their original one. Being relics of a preceding age they enable us, these writers thought, to show that a series of social stages which has been worked out by logical criteria is in fact an historical series; and the order of stages being so determined we can attempt to estimate what were the influences which caused development from one stage to the next. For example, Robertson Smith considered, like McLennan before him, that the custom of the levirate is evidence of a preceding state of society in which polyandry was practised. Likewise, Morgan thought that classificatory systems of kinship nomenclature in which a man calls all male kinsmen of his father's generation 'father' and all kinswomen of his mother's generation 'mother', the children of these people 'brother' and 'sister', and their children 'son' and 'daughter', were evidence that sex relations in these societies were at one time more or less promiscuous.

When we turn to the treatment of religion by nineteenth-century anthropologists we find the same aim and method exemplified, though here, as I have mentioned, there is generally a blend of speculations of both an historical and a psychological kind, assumptions about human nature being introduced into the argument. Thus Sir Edward Tylor (1832–1917), who on the whole was more cautious and critical than most of his contemporaries and avoided their stage-making proclivities, tried to show that all religious belief and cult have developed from certain mistaken inferences from observation of such phenomena as dreams, trances, visions, disease, waking and sleeping, and life and death.

Sir James Frazer (1854–1941), whose literary talent first introduced social anthropology to the general reading public, was another great believer in sociological laws. He postulated three stages of development through which all societies pass: magic, religion, and science. According to him, early man was dominated by magic, which, like science, views nature as 'a series of events occurring in an invariable order without the intervention of personal agency.'[1] But though the magician, like the scientist, assumes laws of nature, a knowledge of which he believes enables him to influence it for his own ends, they are in his case not real, but imaginary, laws. In course of time the more intelligent members of society came to see that this was so, and in the resulting state of disillusionment they conceived of spiritual beings with powers superior to man's, who could be induced by propitiation to alter the course of nature to his advantage. This is the stage of religion. Eventually this was also seen to be an illusion and man entered the final, the scientific, stage of his development.

These Victorian anthropologists were men of outstanding ability, wide learning, and obvious integrity. If they over-emphasized resemblances in custom and belief and paid insufficient attention to diversities, they were investigating a real, and not an imaginary, problem when they attempted to account for remarkable similarities in societies widely separated in space and time; and much of permanent value has come out of their researches. Their use of the comparative method allowed them to separate the general from the particular, and so to classify social phenomena.

Thus to Morgan we owe the inception of the comparative study of kinship systems which has since become so important a part of anthropological research. McLennan not only brought together a great mass of evidence to show how common is the rite of marriage by capture in the wedding ceremonies of the simpler societies, but he was also the first to show that exogamy (he invented the

[1] Sir J. G. Frazer, *The Golden Bough. The Magic Art*, 3rd ed., 1922, vol. I, p. 51.

word) and totemism are widespread features of primitive societies and thereby to give us two of our most important concepts; and to him and to Bachofen is due the credit of being the first to draw attention, against the overwhelming bias in favour of patriarchal origins of the family at that time, to the existence of matrilineal societies in all parts of the world, and of recognizing their great sociological importance. Tylor, among many other achievements, showed the universality of animistic beliefs and established the term animism in our vocabulary. Frazer likewise showed the universality of magical beliefs and that their logical structure can be reduced by analysis to two elementary types, homoeopathic magic and contagious magic; and he brought together a great number of examples of divine kingship and of other institutions and customs, and by so doing brought them into relief as widespread social and cultural patterns.

Moreover, their research was much more critical than that of their predecessors. They had, of course, more knowledge from which to generalize, but, in addition to that, they used their knowledge more systematically than the philosophers, of whom Maine complained: 'The inquiries of the jurist are in truth prosecuted much as inquiry into physics and physiology was prosecuted before observation had taken the place of assumption. Theories, plausible and comprehensive, but absolutely unverified, such as the Law of Nature or the Social Compact, enjoy a universal preference over sober research into the primitive history of society and law.'[1]

Philosophical speculations were of little value when unsupported by factual evidence. It was the 'sober research' of Maine and his contemporaries that opened a way to an understanding of social institutions. Their sifting and classification of the material provided an indispensable corpus of ethnographic fact, hitherto lacking, from

[1] *Ancient Law*, 1912 ed., p. 3.

33

which significant theoretical conclusions could be, and were, drawn and by which they could be tested.

Another virtue found in most of the nineteenth-century writers I have mentioned was that they studied institutions sociologically, in terms of social structure, and not in terms of individual psychology. They avoided arguing deductively, as the philosophers often did, from postulates about human nature, and attempted to explain institutions in terms of other institutions found with them in the same society at the same time or at an earlier period of its history.

Thus when McLennan sought to understand exogamy, he explicitly rejected a biological or psychological determinant of the incest taboo and tried to explain it by reference to the customs of female infanticide and the blood feud and to totemic beliefs. He did not look in human nature for an explanation of the rite of marriage by capture but showed how it can be related to rules of exogamy and how it might be a survival of actual rapine. Likewise he suggested how patriliny might have developed out of matriliny through a combination of the customs of polyandry and patrilocality; and how the worship of animal gods and plant gods and their symbols, and their hierarchical relationship to one another, among the Jews, in India, and in ancient Greece and Rome might have developed out of totemism and a totemic tribal structure.

McLennan rigidly adhered to the thesis that social institutions are functionally interdependent. For instance, he tells us that 'a full explanation of the origin of exogamy requires it to be made out that wherever exogamy prevailed, totemism prevailed; that where totemism prevailed, blood-feuds prevailed; that where blood-feuds prevailed, the religious obligation of vengeance prevailed; that where the religious obligation of vengeance prevailed, female infanticide prevailed; that where female infanticide prevailed, female kinship prevailed. A failure to make good any one of these particulars would be fatal to the entire argument.'[1]

Maine, likewise, was interested in sociological questions—such as the relation of law to religion and morality, the social effects of the codification of law in various historical circumstances, the effect of the development of Rome as a military empire on the legal authority of the father in the family, the relation between the *patria postestas* and agnation, and the movement in progressive societies from law based on status to law based on contract. In his treatment of such problems Maine was forthright in advocating a sociological method of analysis and in condemning what would today be called psychological explanations. 'What mankind did in the primitive state', he argues, 'may not be a hopeless subject of inquiry, but of their motives for doing it it is impossible to know anything. These sketches of the plight of human beings in the first ages of the world are effected by first supposing mankind to be divested of a great part of the circumstances by which they are now surrounded, and then by assuming that, in the condition thus imagined, they would preserve the same sentiments and prejudices by which they are now actuated,—although, in fact, these sentiments may have been created and engendered by those very circumstances of which, by the hypothesis, they are to be stripped.'[2]

In other words, primitive institutions cannot be interpreted in terms of the mentality of the civilized inquirer into them because his mentality is a product of a different set of institutions. To suppose otherwise is to fall into what has been called 'the psychologists' fallacy', so often to be denounced later by Durkheim, Lévy-Bruhl, and other French sociologists.

[1] *Studies in Ancient History* (The Second Series), 1896, p. 28.
[2] *Ancient Law*, 1912 ed., pp. 266–7.

I am not suggesting that the theories of these Victorian anthropologists were sound. For the most part they are not accepted by any anthropologist today, and some of them now appear to be silly not only in the light of our present knowledge but also in the light of the knowledge available at the time they were put forward. Nor am I upholding the method of interpretation. I am merely trying to estimate the significance of these writers for an understanding of the social anthropology of the present day. To appreciate it, and them, we must, I think, bear in mind that the social changes taking place in Europe at the time directed the attention of many thinkers, particularly of philosophers of history, economists, and statisticians, to the role in history of masses, rather than of individuals, and of broad trends, rather than of particular events, and led them to the quest of uniformities and regularities.[1] The study of institutions lent itself easily to this approach, especially when the institutions were those of early man, for which only the outline and direction of development could be surmised, and not the part played in it by individuals or by accidental events, inasmuch as these could not be reconstructed by the comparative method or any other.

But although in some respects these nineteenth-century anthropologists had much the same point of view as those of today, in other respects it differed widely, so widely that it is often difficult for us to read their theoretical constructions without irritation; and at times we feel embarrassed at what seems complacency. In part the difficulty lies in the changes which have taken place in the content of the words used, due, in addition to a general change in outlook, to changes in the meaning of concepts brought about by increase of knowledge; for it must be understood that very little indeed was then

[1] G. P. Gooch, *History and Historians in the Nineteenth Century*, 1949, Chap. XXVIII *et passim*.

known about primitive societies and what were taken for facts were often not facts at all but superficial observations or prejudiced opinion. But even if we make allowance for that, we see now that their use of the comparative method for the purpose of historical reconstructions led them into unjustifiable, and totally unverifiable, conclusions.

These anthropologists of the last century considered that they were writing history, the history of early man, and they were interested in primitive societies not so much in themselves as for the use they could make of them in the hypothetical reconstruction of the earliest history of mankind in general and of their own institutions in particular. Maine's *Ancient Law* has the sub-title *Its Connection with the Early History of Society, and its Relation to Modern Ideas.* The title of Tylor's first book was *Researches into the Early History of Mankind.* Sir John Lubbock's contribution to these studies was called *The Origin of Civilization.* McLennan's essays were brought together in two volumes as *Studies in Ancient History.*

It is not surprising that they wrote what they regarded as history, for all contemporaneous learning was radically historical. The genetic approach, which had borne impressive fruits in philology, was apparent in law, theology, economics, philosophy, and science.[1] There was everywhere a passionate endeavour to discover the origins of everything—the origin of species, the origin of religion, the origin of law, and so on—an endeavour, almost an obsession, to explain always the nearer by the farther.[2]

I mention briefly a few of the major objections to the method pursued in these attempts to explain institutions by seeking to reconstruct their development from supposed origins, for it is important that it should be under-

---

[1] Lord Acton, *A Lecture on the Study of History*, 1895, pp. 56–8.

[2] Marc Bloch, *Apologie pour L'Histoire ou Métier d'Historien*, 1949, p. 5.

stood why social anthropologists in England have turned away from the kind of interpretations set forth by their predecessors.

We would, I think unanimously, hold today that an institution is not to be understood, far less explained, in terms of its origins, whether these origins are conceived of as beginnings, causes, or merely, in a logical sense, its simplest forms. To understand an institution one is certainly aided by knowing its development and the circumstances of its development, but a knowledge of its history cannot of itself tell us how it functions in social life. To know how it has come to be what it is, and to know how it works, are two different things, a distinction I shall discuss further in my next lecture.

But in the case of these nineteenth-century anthropologists we are not offered critical history, not even as it was understood in the middle of the century, when it was still regarded as a literary art and was in no way the systematic study of sources it has become today. Even then history was at least based on documents and monuments totally lacking for reconstruction of the development of the institutions of early man. In that field historical reconstruction had to be almost entirely conjectural, and it was often little more than plausible guesswork. If one accepts that man is descended from some ape-like creature it may be reasonable to suppose that at one time his sexual relations must have been in some degree promiscuous, and to ask further how it has come about that monogamous marriage has developed from this condition; but the supposition and reconstruction of development are purely speculative. They are not history.

It must be noted also that the comparative method, even when it was used merely to establish correlations, without attempting further to give them a chronological value, had, when applied to social institutions, serious weaknesses which not even the learning and industry of Tylor, or the statistical methods he summoned to his aid, could overcome. The facts submitted to analysis were generally inaccurate or insufficient, and they were also often wrenched from the social contexts which alone gave them meaning. Furthermore, it was found exceedingly difficult, if not impossible, when dealing with complex social phenomena to establish the units to be submitted to analysis by the method of concomitant variations. It is easy to ask how constantly are totemism and clans found together but it is very difficult to define 'totemism' and 'clan' for the purpose of the inquiry. It is even more difficult to give precise definition to such concepts as 'property', 'crime', 'monogamy', 'democracy', 'slavery' and many other terms.

A further difficulty in these investigations, complicated by the spread of institutions and ideas, was to decide what was to be regarded as an instance of the occurrence of a social fact. Does the occurrence of polygamy throughout the Muslim world count as one instance of polygamy or as many? Are parliamentary institutions derived from, and modelled on, the British system in many parts of the world to count as one instance of them or as many?

It will be clear to you from what I have already said that in two important respects nineteenth-century anthropology differed from that of today. It sought to interpret institutions by showing how they might have originated and by what steps they might have developed. We may here leave for further consideration the question of the relevance of historical development for sociological inquiry where the history is known. Most of us would certainly take the view that, since the history of the institutions of primitive peoples is not known, a systematic study of them as they are at the present time must precede any attempt at conjecturing how they may have originated and developed. We would also hold that how they originated and developed is in any case a problem which, however relevant to the problem of how they function in society, is a different problem and one that has to be separately investigated by a different technique.

Another way of expressing this point would be to say that social anthropology and ethnology were regarded by the nineteenth-century anthropologists as a single discipline whereas they are regarded today as distinct.

The second main difference I would like to draw your attention to is only now beginning to emerge clearly in anthropology. In my first lecture I referred to the difference between culture and society. This distinction was scarcely made by the anthropologists of last century. Had they made it, most of them would have regarded culture, and not social relations, as the subject matter of their inquiries; and culture was for them something concrete. They thought of exogamy, totemism, matriliny, ancestor worship, slavery, and so forth as customs—things—and it was an inquiry into these customs, or things, that they regarded themselves as pursuing. Consequently their concepts had always to carry such a heavy load of cultural reality that comparative analysis was bogged down at the outset.

It was not till the end of the century that anthropologists began to classify societies on the basis of their social structures, rather than of their cultures, as a first essential step towards making comparative studies profitable. Social anthropology besides having now separated itself from ethnology has also defined its subject matter as social relations, rather than culture, and has consequently been able to reach a clearer appreciation of its problems and to fashion a method of inquiry into them. Its method is still a comparative method, but it is used for a different purpose and in a different way, and what it compares is different.

Apart from these differences in method one feels also a

moral separation from the anthropologists of last century —or at least I do. Their reconstructions were not only conjectural but evaluatory. Liberals and rationalists, they believed above all in progress, the kind of material, political, social, and philosophical changes which were taking place in Victorian England. Industrialism, democracy, science, and so forth were good in themselves. Consequently the explanations of social institutions they put forward amount, when examined, to little more than hypothetical scales of progress, at one end of which were placed forms of institutions or beliefs as they were in nineteenth-century Europe and America, while at the other end were placed their antitheses. An order of stages was then worked out to show what logically might have been the history of development from one end of the scale to the other. All that remained to be done was to hunt through ethnological literature for examples to illustrate each of these stages. For all their insistence on empiricism in the study of social institutions, the nineteenth-century anthropologists were therefore hardly less dialectical, speculative, and dogmatic than the moral philosophers of the preceding century, even though they felt that they had to support their constructions with a wealth of factual evidence, a need scarcely felt by the moral philosophers.

We are less certain today about the values they accepted. In part, at any rate, the turning away from the construction of stages of development which so occupied them, and the turning towards inductive functional studies of primitive societies, must be attributed to the growth of scepticism whether many of the changes taking place in the nineteenth century can be wholly regarded as improvement; for, whatever the opinion of those who pursue it may be, modern social anthropology is conservative in its theoretical approach. Its interests are more in what makes for integration and equilibrium in society than in plotting scales and stages of progress.

However, I think that the major cause of confusion among nineteenth-century anthropologists was not so much that they believed in progress and sought a method by which they might reconstruct how it had come about, for they were well aware that their schemata were hypotheses which could not be finally or fully verified. It is rather to be looked for in the assumption they had inherited from the Enlightenment that societies are natural systems, or organisms, which have a necessary course of development that can be reduced to general principles or laws. Logical connections were in consequence presented as real and necessary connections and typological classifications as both historical and inevitable courses of development. It will readily be seen how a combination of the notion of scientific law and that of progress leads in anthropology, as in the philosophy of history, to procrustean stages, the presumed inevitability of which gives them a normative quality. Naturally, those who believed that social life could be reduced to scientific laws concluded that similar forms of institutions must have sprung from similar forms and they from similar prototypes. In my next lecture I shall discuss this point further and in relation to the social anthropology of today.

III

LATER THEORETICAL
DEVELOPMENTS

In my last lecture I gave you an account of the main characteristics of the writers of the eighteenth and nineteenth centuries who can be regarded in some measure as having studied social institutions in an anthropological way. In both centuries the approach was naturalistic and empirical in intention, if not in practice; generalizing, and above all genetic. Their thought was dominated by the notion of progress, of improvement of manners and customs from rudeness to civility, from savagery to civilization; and the method of investigation they elaborated, the comparative method, was chiefly employed by them for the purpose of reconstructing the hypothetical course of this development. It is in this respect that the anthropology of today is most at variance with that of yesterday.

The reaction against the attempt to explain social institutions by their reconstructed past, to explain what we know something about by what we know next to nothing about, came at the end of last century; and it was particularly directed against those schemes of parallel, seen ideally as unilinear, development which had been so much in favour. Though this genetic anthropology, often, but unfortunately, called evolutionary anthropology, was recast and re-presented in the writings of Steinmetz, Nieboer, Westermarck, Hobhouse,[1] and

[1] S. R. Steinmetz, *Ethnologische Studien zur ersten Entwicklung der Strafe*, 1894; H. J. Nieboer, *Slavery as an Industrial System*, 1900; Edward Westermarck, *The Origin and Development of the Moral Ideas*, 1906; L. T. Hobhouse, *Morals in Evolution*, 1906.

others, it had finally lost its appeal. Some anthropologists, and in varying degrees, now turned for inspiration to psychology, which at the time seemed to provide satisfactory solutions of many of their problems without recourse to hypothetical history. This attempt to construct social anthropology on the foundations of psychology has proved to be, then and since, an attempt to build a house on shifting sands.

There is an undercurrent of psychological assumptions in the stream of anthropological theory in the eighteenth and nineteenth centuries, but though assumptions about human nature were made, and inevitably made, by the writers of the time they did not suggest that customs and institutions could be understood by reference to individual feelings and impulses. Indeed, as we have seen, they often explicitly rejected the suggestion. It must be remembered that there was not at that time anything which could be called experimental psychology, so that when anthropologists even as recent as Tylor and Frazer looked to psychology for aid it was to associationist psychology that they looked; and when this kind of psychology went out of fashion they were left in the outmoded intellectualist interpretations they derived from it.

Other anthropologists were later left in a similar way in the fashion of introspective psychology. I am thinking particularly of writings on such subjects as religion, magic, taboo, and witchcraft—by Marett, Malinowski and others in this country, and by Lowie, Radin, and a number of other anthropologists in America.[1] These writers all, in one way or another, tried to account for social behaviour pertaining to the sacred in terms of feelings or emotional states—of hate, greed, love, fear,

[1] R. R. Marett, *The Threshold of Religion*, 1909; B. Malinowski, 'Magic, Science and Religion', *Science, Religion and Reality*, 1925; R. H. Lowie, *Primitive Religion*, 1925; Paul Radin, *Social Anthropology*, 1932.

44

awe, amazement, a sense of the mysterious or extra-
ordinary, wonder, projection of will, and so on. The
behaviour arises in situations of emotional stress,
frustration, or intensity and its function is cathartic,
expletive, or stimulating. The development of various
modern experimental psychologies showed all such interpretations to be confused, irrelevant, or meaningless.
Nevertheless, undeterred by the fate of their predecessors,
some anthropologists, especially in America, now attempt
to state their findings in that mixture of behaviouristic
and psycho-analytical psychologies which is called personality psychology or the psychology of motivations and
attitudes.

There are various and particular objections to each of
these successive attempts to explain social facts by individual psychology; and there is one common objection
to all of them. Psychology and social anthropology study
different kinds of phenomena and what the one studies
cannot therefore be understood in terms of conclusions
reached by the other. Psychology is the study of individual
life. Social anthropology is the study of social life.
Psychology studies psychical systems. Social anthropology
studies social systems. The psychologist and the social
anthropologist may observe the same acts of raw behaviour but they study them at different levels of
abstraction.

Let me give you a simple example. A man on trial
for a crime is found guilty by twelve jurymen and is
sentenced by a judge to be punished. The facts of
sociological significance are here the existence of a law,
the various legal institutions and procedures brought into
play by a breach of it, and the action of the political
society through its representatives in punishing the
criminal. Throughout the process the thoughts and
feelings of the accused, the jurymen, and the judge
would be found to vary in kind and degree and at differ-

ent times, just as their ages and the colour of their hair and eyes would be found to vary, but these variations would not be of any concern, or at any rate not of any immediate concern, to the social anthropologist. He is not interested in the actors in the drama as individuals but as persons who play certain roles in the process of justice. On the other hand, to the psychologist, who is studying individuals, the feelings, motives, opinions, and so forth, of the actors are of first importance and the legal procedures and processes of secondary interest. This essential difference between social anthropology and psychology is the *pons asinorum* in the learning of social anthropology. The two disciplines can only be of value —and they can be of great value—to each other if each pursues independently its own research into its own problems and by its own methods.

Apart from the criticisms of the so-called evolutionary theories of nineteenth-century anthropology implied in the ignoring of them by those who sought psychological explanations of customs and beliefs, these theories were attacked from two directions, the diffusionist and the functionalist.

The criticisms of those who became known as diffusionist anthropologists were based on the very obvious fact that culture is often borrowed and does not emerge in similar forms in different societies by spontaneous growth due to certain common social potentialities and common human nature. Where we know the history of an invention, whether in technology, art, thought, or custom, we almost invariably find that it has not been made independently by a number of peoples in different places and at different times but by one people in one place and at a particular moment of their history, and that it has spread, wholly or in part, from this people to other peoples. When we look into the matter further we find that there have been a limited number of centres of important cultural development and diffusion, and also that in the process of borrowing and incorporation into other cultures the diffused traits may undergo all sorts of modifications and changes. Since it can be shown that the inventions for the history of which we have reliable evidence have almost invariably diffused in this manner it is not unreasonable to suppose, when we find similar artifacts, ideas, and customs among primitive peoples in different parts of the world, that these have in the same way spread from a limited number of points of cultural advancement, even though there is no other evidence of their having done so than that contained in their similarity and their geographical distribution; especially if the traits are at all complex and are also found in association.

The bearing of this argument on the genetic theories of the anthropologists of last century, which it did so much to discredit, is obvious. If it could be shown that an institution of some people had through the accidents of history been taken over by them from another people it could then hardly be regarded as a natural and inevitable development of their previous institutions and cited as evidence of some law of growth.

Diffusionist anthropology is still predominant in America. In England it had little lasting influence, partly on account of its uncritical use by Elliot Smith, Perry and Rivers,[1] but also partly because its reconstructions were just as conjectural and unverifiable as the genetic reconstructions it attacked; and the functionalist anthropologists, to whom I now turn, regarded the fight between evolutionists and diffusionists as a family quarrel between ethnologists and none of their affair.

The functionalist objection to both was not only that

[1] G. Elliot Smith, *The Ancient Egyptians*, 1911; W. J. Perry, *The Children of the Sun*, 1923; W. H. R. Rivers, *The History of Melanesian Society*, 1914.

their reconstructions were guesswork, but also that they were trying to explain social life in terms of the past. This is not the procedure of natural scientists, which most writers of this persuasion—and that means most English social anthropologists—consider themselves to be. To understand how an aeroplane or the human body works one studies the first in the light of the laws of mechanics and the second in the light of the laws of physiology. One need not know anything about the history of aeronautics or the theory of biological evolution. Likewise a language can be studied from various angles—grammar, phonetics, semantics, and so forth—without the history of its words having to be known. The history of its words belongs to a different branch of linguistics, philology. In the same way, a history of the legal institutions of the England of today will only show us how they have come to be what they are and not how they function in our social life. To understand how they work requires a study by the experimental methods of the natural sciences. Historical and natural science studies are different kinds of study with different aims, methods, and techniques, and only confusion can result from trying to pursue both together.

In the study of primitive societies it is the task of the historian of primitive peoples, the ethnologist, to discover, if he can, how their institutions have come to be what they are. It is the task of the scientist, the social anthropologist, to discover their functions in the social systems to which they belong. Even with the best sources at his disposal, the historian can only tell us what has been the succession of accidental events by which a society has become what it is. These events could not be deduced from general principles, nor can a study of the events yield them. The nineteenth-century anthropologists were therefore doubly at fault; they were reconstructing history without adequate material for doing so, and they were seeking to establish sociological laws by a method which cannot lead to their establishment. The general acceptance of this position separated social anthropology from ethnology and gave to social anthropology its present autonomy in the wider study of man.

In making these assertions, social anthropologists are maintaining that societies are natural systems of which all the parts are interdependent, each serving in a complex of necessary relations to maintain the whole, and that social life can be reduced to scientific laws which allow prediction. There are here several propositions. The two basic ones, which I shall briefly examine, can be resumed into the statements that societies are systems, and that these systems are natural systems which can be reduced to variables, with the corollary that the history of them is irrelevant to an inquiry into their nature.

That there is some kind of order, consistency and constancy, in social life is obvious. If there were not, none of us would be able to go about our affairs or satisfy our most elementary needs. It will at once also be seen that this order is brought about by the systematization, or institutionalization, of social activities so that certain persons have certain roles in them and so that the activities have certain functions in the general social life. To take an example we have used earlier—in a Court of Criminal Law the judge, the jurymen, the barristers, the clerks, the policemen and the accused, have definite roles, and the action of the Court as a whole has the functions of establishing guilt and punishing crime. The individuals occupying these positions vary from case to case but the form and functions of the institution are constant. It is also obvious that the judge, the barristers, the clerks, and the policemen have professional roles' which they can only carry out if there is some economic organization so that they do not, for example, have to grow and prepare their own food but can buy it with the remuneration they receive for the performance of their duties; and also if

there is some political organization which maintains law
and order, so that they have security in the performance
of their duties; and so forth.

All this is so.evident that the ideas of social system,
social structure, social roles, and the social functions of
institutions are found in one form or another in the
earliest philosophical reflections on social life. Without
going back beyond the names I mentioned in my last
lecture, we note that the concepts of structure and
function appear in Montaigne's use of the terms *basti-
ment* and *liaison* in his discussion of law and custom in
general, which he compares to 'a structure of different
pieces joined together, so connected that it is impossible
to disturb one without the whole body feeling it'.[1] The
same concept of social system, of which the idea of social
function is part, is present throughout Montesquieu's
discussion of the nature and principles of different types
of society, in which he speaks of the *structure* of a society
and the *rapports* between its parts; and we find it, to a
greater or lesser degree, in all the eighteenth-century
philosophers who wrote about social institutions. In the
early nineteenth century it is clearly enunciated by
Comte, and though not always explicitly formulated, and
though subordinated to the concepts of origin, cause,
and stages of development, it is subsumed by all the
anthropological writers of that century. Towards the
end of it, and increasingly during the present century,
greater emphasis was laid on the concept in harmony
with a general orientation of thought. Just as earlier the
genetic approach was dominant in all fields of learning,
so now we find everywhere a functional orientation.
There were functional biology, functional psychology,
functional law, functional economics, and so forth, as
well as functional anthropology.

[1] 'De la Coustume et de ne Changer aisément une Loy Receüe', *Essais*,
Nouvelle Revue Française, Bibliothèque de la Pléiade, 1946, p. 132.

The two writers who most specifically directed the attention of social anthropologists towards functional analysis were Herbert Spencer and Emile Durkheim. The philosophical writings of Herbert Spencer (1820–1903) are little read today, but during his life-time they had great influence. He and Comte were alike in their versatility, both attempting to cover the whole of human knowledge and within it to construct a comprehensive science of society and culture, what Spencer called the super-organic.[1] In his view the evolution of human society, though not necessarily of particular societies, is a natural and inevitable continuation of organic evolution. Groups tend always towards increase in size and consequently in organization and therefore in integration, since the greater the structural differentiation the greater is the interdependence of the parts of the social organism. Spencer's use of the biological analogy of organism, dangerous though it has proved to be, did much to further the use of the concepts of structure and function in social anthropology, for he constantly stressed that at every stage in social evolution there is a necessary functional interdependence between the institutions of a society, which must always tend towards a state of equilibrium if it is to persist. He was also a great advocate of sociological laws, both structural and genetic.

The writings of Emile Durkheim (1858–1917) had a greater and more direct influence on social anthropology. Indeed he is a central figure in the history of its development, both on account of his general sociological theories and because he and a band of talented colleagues and pupils applied them with remarkable insight to the study of primitive societies.[2]

[1] *The Study of Sociology*, 1872 onwards; *The Principles of Sociology*, 1882-3.

[2] His best known works are *De la Division du Travail Social: Etude sur L'organisation des Sociétés Supérieures*, 1893; *Les Règles de la Méthode*

Briefly, Durkheim's position was as follows: Social facts cannot be explained in terms of individual psychology, if only because they exist outside and apart from individual minds. A language, for example, is there before an individual is born into the society which speaks it, and it will be there after he is dead. He merely learns to speak it, as his ancestors did, and as his descendants will. It is a social fact, something *sui generis*, which can only be understood in its relation to other facts of the same order, that is to say as part of a social system and in terms of its functions in the maintenance of that system.

Social facts are characterized by their generality, their transmissibility, and their compulsion. All members of a society have, in general, the same habits and customs, language, and morals, and all live in the same common framework of legal, political, and economic institutions. All these things form a more or less stable structure which persists in its essentials over great periods of time, being handed down from generation to generation. The individual merely passes through the structure, as it were. It was not born with him and it does not die with him, for it is not a psychical system but a social system with a collective consciousness quite different in kind from individual consciousness. The totality of social facts which compose the structure are obligatory. The individual who does not abide by them always suffers penalties and disabilities of a legal or moral kind. Usually he has neither the desire nor the opportunity to do other than conform. A child born in France of French parents can only learn French and has no desire to do otherwise.

In emphaṣizing the singularity of collective life

Sociologique, 1895; *La Suicide: Etude de Sociologie*, 1897; and *Les Formes Elémentaires de la Vie Religieuse: Le Système Totémique en Australie*, 1912. See also many articles and review-articles in *L'Année Sociologique* from 1898 onwards, and those by Hubert, Mauss, and others in the same journal.

Durkheim has been much criticized for holding that there is a collective mind but, although his writing is sometimes rather metaphysical, he certainly never conceived of any such entity. By what he called 'collective representations' he meant what we in England would call a common body of values and beliefs and customs which the individual born into any society learns, accepts, lives by, and passes on. A brilliant study of the ideological content of those collective representations was made by his colleague Lucien Lévy-Bruhl (1857–1939) in a series of books which have had considerable influence in England, though they have been much misunderstood and severely criticized by English anthropologists.[1] Taking for granted that the beliefs, myths, and in general, the ideas, of primitive peoples are a reflection of their social structures and therefore differ from one kind of society to another, he devoted himself to showing how they form systems, the logical principle of which is what he called the law of mystical participation. This was as much a structural analysis as the work of Durkheim, but whereas Durkheim analysed social activities Lévy-Bruhl analysed the ideas associated with them.

Durkheim's importance in the history of the conceptual development of social anthropology in this country might have been no greater than it has been in America had it not been for the influence of his writings on Professor A. R. Radcliffe-Brown and the late Professor B. Malinowski, the two men who have shaped social anthropology into what it is in England today. All of us now teaching the subject in England and in the Dominions are directly or indirectly, for the most part directly, their pupils.

I shall say more about Malinowski (1884–1942) later, especially in my lecture on fieldwork, for if functional

[1] His two best known works are *Les Fonctions Mentales dans les Sociétés Inférieures*, 1912, and *La Mentalité Primitive*, 1922.

anthropology meant more to him than a principle of field techniques it was as a literary device for integrating his observations for descriptive purposes. It was not, properly speaking, a methodological concept, and he never showed himself capable of using it with any clarity when dealing with the abstractions of general theory. Professor Radcliffe-Brown has far more clearly and consistently stated the functional, or organismic, theory of society. He has presented it in a systematic form and with clarity of exposition and lucidity of style.

Professor Radcliffe-Brown tells us that 'the concept of function applied to human societies is based on an analogy between social life and organic life.'[1] Following Durkheim, he defines the function of a social institution as the correspondence between the social institution and the necessary conditions of existence of the social organism; function used in this sense being—I quote Professor Radcliffe-Brown again—'the contribution which a partial activity makes to the total activity of which it is a part. The function of a particular social usage is the contribution it makes to the total social life as the functioning of the total social system.'[2]

Institutions are thus thought of as functioning within a social structure consisting of individual human beings 'connected by a definite set of social relations into an integrated whole'.[3] The continuity of the structure is maintained by the process of social life or, in other words, the social life of a community is the functioning of its structure. So conceived of, a social system has a functional unity. It is not an aggregate but an organism or integrated whole.

Professor Radcliffe-Brown says that when he speaks of social integration he assumes that 'the function of culture

[1] 'On the Concept of Function in Social Science', *American Anthropologist*, 1935, p. 394.
[2] Ibid., p. 397.　　　　　　　　　　[3] Ibid., p. 396.

as a whole is to unite individual human beings into more or less stable social structures, i.e., stable systems of groups determining and regulating the relation of those individuals to one another, and providing such external adaptation to the physical environment, and such internal adaptation between the component individuals or groups, as to make possible an ordered social life. That assumption I believe to be a sort of primary postulate of any objective and scientific study of culture or of human society.'[1]

The elaboration of the concepts of social structure, social system, and social function as defined by Professor Radcliffe-Brown in the last quotation, and as used by social anthropologists today, has been an important aid in the determination of problems of field research. The nineteenth-century anthropologists were content to let laymen collect the facts on which they based their theories, and it did not occur to them that there was any need for them to make studies of primitive peoples themselves. This was because they were dealing atomistically with items of culture, customs, which could be brought together to show either the great similarity or the great diversity of beliefs and practices, or to illustrate stages in human progress. But once it was accepted that a custom is more or less meaningless when taken out of its social context it became apparent both that comprehensive and detailed studies of primitive peoples in every aspect of their social life would have to be undertaken, and that they could only be undertaken by professional social anthropologists who were aware of the theoretical problems in the subject, had in mind the kind of information required for the solution of them, and were alone able to put themselves in the position where it could be acquired.

[1] 'The Present Position of Anthropological Studies', Presidential Address, *British Association for the Advancement of Science*, Section H., 1931, p. 13.

The functionalist insistence on the relatedness of things has thus been partly responsible for, as it has been partly the product of, modern field studies. I shall discuss this aspect of modern social anthropology in my next two lectures.

Functional anthropology, with its emphasis on the concept of social system and hence on the need for systematic studies of the social life of primitive peoples as they are today, thus not only separated, as we have seen, social anthropology from ethnology; it also brought together the theoretical study of institutions and the observational study of primitive social life. We have noted how in the eighteenth century philosophical speculations about the nature and origins of social institutions were occasionally illustrated by reports of explorers about rude societies. We saw then how in the nineteenth century these primitive societies in themselves became the chief object of curiosity of a few scholars interested in the development of culture and institutions, but who relied exclusively on the observations of others, the theoretical thinker and the observer still being divorced. In functional anthropology the two were, as I shall explain more in detail in my next lecture, finally united, and social anthropology in the modern sense of the words came into existence as a distinctive discipline in which theoretical problems of general sociology are investigated by research in primitive societies.

The functional approach had the further effect of changing both the purpose and the use of the comparative method. We saw that the older anthropologists regarded the comparative method as a means of making historical reconstructions in the absence of recorded history, and that the way they used it was to compare examples of particular customs or institutions gathered haphazardly from all over the world. Once the notion of system is accepted as a primary postulate, as Professor

Radcliffe-Brown calls it, the object of research ceases to be ethnological classification and the elaboration of cultural categories and schemes of hypothetical development. It becomes in studies of particular societies the definition of social activities in terms of their functions within their social systems, and in comparative studies a comparison of institutions as parts of social systems or in the relation they have to the whole life of the societies in which they are found. What the modern anthropologist compares are not customs, but systems of relations. This is another matter about which I shall have something further to say in later lectures.

I now come to the second postulate of functional anthropology, that social systems are natural systems which can be reduced to sociological laws, with the corollary that the history of them has no scientific relevance. I must confess that this seems to me to be doctrinaire positivism at its worst. One has a right, I think, to ask those who assert that the aim of social anthropology is to formulate sociological laws similar to the laws formulated by natural scientists to produce formulations which resemble what are called laws in these sciences. Up to the present nothing even remotely resembling what are called laws in the natural sciences has been adduced—only rather naïve deterministic, teleological, and pragmatic assertions. The generalizations which have so far been attempted have, moreover, been so vague and general as to be, even if true, of little use, and they have rather easily tended to become mere tautologies and platitudes on the level of common sense deduction.

Such being the case, I think that we may ask again whether social systems are in fact natural systems at all, whether, for instance, a legal system is really comparable to a physiological system or the planetary system. I cannot see myself that there is any good reason for regarding a social system as a system of the same kind as an organic or inorganic system. It seems to me to be an entirely different kind of system; and I think that the effort to discover natural laws of society is vain and leads only to airy discussions about methods. Anyhow, I am not obliged to prove that there are no such laws; it is for those who say that there are, to tell us what they are.

Those of us who take the view I have expressed about this issue must ask ourselves whether the functionalist claim that the history of an institution is irrelevant to an understanding of it as it is at the present time is acceptable, for the claim rests precisely on a conception of system and law in reference to human affairs which is at variance with our own. A brief consideration of this question will give me the opportunity to outline my own position, for I do not want it to be thought that, in criticizing some of the underlying assumptions of functionalism, I do not regard myself as in other respects a functionalist and follower in the footsteps of my teachers, Professor Malinowski and Professor Radcliffe-Brown, or that I hold that societies are not intelligible and cannot be systematically studied, or that no significant general statements of any kind can be made about them.

In speaking here of history I am not now discussing ethnological hypotheses, whether of a genetic or a diffusionist kind. We may regard that issue as closed. I am discussing the relevance to a study of social institutions of the history of them where this history is known for certain and in detail. This problem was hardly seen by the eighteenth-century moral philosophers and their Victorian successors, because it did not occur to them that the study of institutions could be anything else than a study of their development, the final aim of their labours being a comprehensive natural history of human society.

Sociological laws were consequently conceived of by them as laws of progress. Without the quest for laws— for in that matter American anthropologists are as sceptical as I am—anthropology in the United States is still for the most part historical in its aims. It is for that reason regarded as being more ethnology than social anthropology by functionalist anthropologists in England, who take the view that it is not the task of social anthropologists to investigate the history of the societies they study, and furthermore that a knowledge of their history does not help us to understand the functioning of their institutions. This attitude follows logically enough from the assumption that societies are natural systems which are to be studied by the methods employed, in so far as they are applicable, by such natural scientists as chemists and biologists.

This is an issue which is coming more to the fore to-day when social anthropologists are beginning to study societies belonging to historical cultures. So long as they were investigating such peoples as Australian aborigines or South Sea Islanders, who have no recorded history, they could ignore history with an easy conscience. Now, however, that they have begun to study peasant communities in India and Europe, Arab nomads, and like communities elsewhere, they can no longer make a virtue of necessity but must choose deliberately to ignore or to take into consideration their social past in making studies of their social present.

Those of us who do not accept the functionalist position in respect of history would hold that, though it is necessary to make separate studies of a society as it is today and of its development in the past and to employ different techniques in each study, and though it may be desirable for these separate studies, at any rate in certain circumstances, to be made by different persons, nevertheless, to know a society's past gives one a deeper

59

understanding of the nature of its social life at the present time; for history is not merely a succession of changes but, as others have said, a growth. The past is contained in the present as the present is in the future. I am not saying that social life can be understood through a knowledge of its past, but that this knowledge gives us a fuller understanding of it than we would have were its past unknown to us. It is also evident that problems of social development can only be studied in terms of history, and furthermore that history alone provides a satisfactory experimental situation in which the hypotheses of functional anthropology can be tested.

Very much more could be said about this question, but you may think that it is a domestic issue which might well be discussed at greater length in a gathering of specialists but is unsuited for detailed argument before a general audience. So, having stated that there is this division of opinion, I will leave the matter there. It is only fair, however, since I have said that I and others, unlike most of our colleagues in this country, regard social anthropology as belonging to the humanities rather than to the natural sciences, that I should tell you what I conceive the method and aim of social anthropology to be.

In my view, it is much more like certain branches of historical scholarship—social history and the history of institutions and of ideas as contrasted with narrative and political history—than it is to any of the natural sciences. The similarity between this kind of historiography and social anthropology has been obscured by the fact that social anthropologists make direct studies of social life whereas historians make indirect studies of it from documentary and other sources; by the fact that social anthropologists study primitive societies which lack recorded history; and by the fact that social anthropologists generally study synchronic problems while historians study diachronic problems. I agree with Professor Kroeber[1] that these are differences of technique, emphasis, and perspective, and not of aim or method, and that essentially the method of both historiography and social anthropology is descriptive integration, even though anthropological synthesis is usually on a higher plane of abstraction than historical synthesis and anthropology more explicitly and deliberately than history aims at comparison and generalization.

As I understand the matter, what the social anthropologist does can be divided into three phases. In the first phase, as ethnographer, he goes to live among a primitive people and learns their way of life. He learns to speak their language, to think in their concepts, and to feel in their values. He then lives the experience over again critically and interpretatively in the conceptual categories and values of his own culture and in terms of the general body of knowledge of his discipline. In other words, he translates from one culture into another.

In the second phase of his work, and still within a single ethnographic study of a particular primitive society, he tries to go beyond this literary and impressionistic stage and to discover the structural order of the society, so that it is intelligible not merely at the level of consciousness and action, as it is to one of its members or to the foreigner who has learnt its mores and participates in its life, but also at the level of sociological analysis.[2] Just as the linguist does not merely learn to understand, speak and translate a native language but seeks to reveal its phonological and grammatical systems, so the social anthropologist is not content merely to

---

[1] A. L. Kroeber, 'History and Science in Anthropology', *American Anthropologist*, 1935.

[2] Claude Lévi-Strauss, 'Histoire et Ethnologie', *Revue de Métaphysique et de Morale*, 1949.

observe and describe the social life of a primitive people but seeks to reveal its underlying structural order, the patterns which, once established, enable him to see it as a whole, as a set of interrelated abstractions.

Having isolated these structural patterns in one society, the social anthropologist, in the third phase of his work, compares them with patterns in other societies. The study of each new society enlarges his knowledge of the range of basic social structures and enables him better to construct a typology of forms, and to determine their essential features and the reasons for their variations.

Most of my colleagues would, I fancy, disagree with this description of what a social anthropologist does. They would prefer to describe what he does in the language of the methodology of the natural sciences, whereas what I have said implies that social anthropology studies societies as moral, or symbolic, systems and not as natural systems, that it is less interested in process than in design, and that it therefore seeks patterns and not laws, demonstrates consistency and not necessary relations between social activities, and interprets rather than explains. These are conceptual and not merely verbal differences.

You have seen that there are a good number of unresolved methodological and, underlying them, philosophical problems in social anthropology: whether psychological interpretations of social facts should or should not be attempted; whether society and culture should be a single field, or separate fields, of inquiry, and what is the relation between these abstractions; what meaning is to be given to such terms as structure, system, and function; and whether social anthropology is to be regarded as an embryonic natural science or is directing its course to a mirage in pursuit of sociological laws. In all these issues we anthropologists are at sixes and sevens among ourselves, and no amount of argument will resolve the differences of opinion. The only arbitrament we all accept is appeal to the facts—to the judgment of research. In my next lecture I will discuss this side to our subject.

IV

FIELDWORK AND THE
EMPIRICAL TRADITION

In my last two lectures I gave you some account of the development of theory in social anthropology. Theory has changed its direction with the increase in knowledge about primitive peoples which it has in each generation been largely responsible for bringing about. It is about this growth of knowledge that I shall speak tonight.

There has always been a popular, though not unhealthy, prejudice against theory as contrasted with experience. However, an established theory is only a generalization from experience which has been again confirmed by it, and a hypothesis is merely an unconfirmed opinion that, judging by what is already known, it is reasonable to assume that further facts will be found by research to be of a certain kind. Without theories and hypotheses anthropological research could not be carried out, for one only finds things, or does not find them, if one is looking for them. Often one finds something other than what one is looking for. The whole history of scholarship, whether in the natural sciences or in the humanities, tells us that the mere collection of what are called facts unguided by theory in observation and selection is of little value.

Nevertheless, one still hears it said of anthropologists that they go to study primitive peoples with a theoretical bias and that this distorts their accounts of savage life, whereas the practical man of affairs, having no such bias, gives an impartial record of the facts as he sees them.

The difference between them is really of another kind. The student makes his observations to answer questions arising out of the generalizations of specialized opinion, and the layman makes his to answer questions arising out of the generalizations of popular opinion. Both have theories, the one systematic and the other popular.

In fact the history of social anthropology may be regarded as the substitution, by slow gradations, of informed opinion about primitive peoples for uninformed opinion, and the stage reached in this process at any time is roughly relative to the amount of organized knowledge available. In the end it is the volume, accuracy, and variety of well authenticated fact which alone counts; and it is the function of theory to stimulate and guide observation in the collection of it. Here, however, I am not so much concerned with popular opinion as with that held by writers about social institutions.

There seems to have been a pendulum swing from extreme to extreme in speculations about primitive man. First he was a little more than an animal who lived in poverty, violence, and fear; then he was a gentle person who lived in plenty, peace, and security. First he was lawless; then he was a slave to law and custom. First he was devoid of any religious feelings or belief; then he was entirely dominated by the sacred and immersed in ritual. First he was an individualist who preyed on the weaker and held what he could; then he was a communist who held lands and goods in common. First he was sexually promiscuous; then he was a model of domestic virtue. First he was lethargic and incorrigibly lazy, then he was alert and industrious. In seeking to change a received opinion it is, I suppose, natural that in the selection and massing of evidence against it an opposite distortion is made.

The dependence of theory on available knowledge in these speculations and the shaping of each by the other may be seen throughout the development of social anthropology. The prevailing opinion about primitive man in the seventeenth and eighteenth centuries, that his life was 'solitary, poore, nasty, brutish, and short', lacked foundation in fact; but it is difficult to see what other conclusion could have been reached from the accounts of contemporary travellers, who for the most part described the primitives they saw in such terms as they have 'nothing that can entitle them to humanity but speech'—this is Sir John Chardin speaking of the Circassians whose country he traversed in 1671[1]—or that they 'differ but little from beasts'—this is Father Stanislaus Arlet speaking about the Indians of Peru in 1698.[2] These early travel accounts, whether they portrayed the savage as brutish or noble, were generally fanciful or mendacious, superficial, and full of inappropriate judgments.

However, it is only fair to say that much depended on the refinement of the traveller and on his temperament and character, and that from the sixteenth century onwards there are not lacking accounts which give sober and factual, if limited, descriptions of native life, such, to mention a few names besides those I have referred to earlier, as the writings of the Englishman Andrew Battel on the natives of the Congo, of the Portuguese Jesuit Father Jerome Lobo on the Abyssinians, of the Dutchman William Bosman on the peoples of the Gold Coast, and of Captain Cook on the natives in the South Seas. They wrote in the spirit of Father Lobo, of whom Dr. Johnson, his translator in *Pinkerton's Voyages*, remarks: 'He appears by his modest and unaffected narration to have described things as he saw them, to have copied

[1] *Pinkerton's Voyages*, vol. IX, 1811, p. 143.
[2] John Lockman, *Travels of the Jesuits*, vol. I, 1743, p. 93.

nature from the life, and to have consulted his senses not his imagination.'[1]

When these early European travellers went beyond description and personal judgments it was generally to establish parallels between the peoples of whom they wrote and the ancients with whom they were familiar from literature, often with the purpose of showing that there must have been some historical influence of the higher cultures on the lower. Father Lafitau thus makes many comparisons between the Huron and Iroquois Redskins and the Jews, the early Christians, the classical Spartans and Cretans, and the ancient Egyptians. In the same manner de la Crequinière, a French traveller to the East Indies in the seventeenth century, sets out to find parallels in India to certain Jewish and classical customs and thus help towards a better understanding of the Scriptures and of the classical writers, for, he says, 'the knowledge of the customs of the Indians, is in no ways useful in itself . . .'[2]

Between the heyday of the moral philosophers and the earliest anthropological writings in a strict sense, between, that is, the middle of the eighteenth century and the middle of the nineteenth century, knowledge of primitive peoples and of the peoples of the Far East was greatly increased. The European colonization of America had been widely expanded, British rule had been established in India, and Australia, New Zealand, and South Africa had been settled by European emigrants. The character of ethnographic description of the peoples of these regions began to change from travellers' tales to detailed studies by missionaries and administrators who not only had better opportunities to observe, but were also men of greater culture than the gentlemen of fortune of earlier times.

[1] *Pinkerton's Voyages*, vol. XV, 1814, p. 1.

[2] *Customs of the East Indians*, 1705, p. viii. (Translated from *Conformité des Coutumes des Indiens Orientaux*, 1704, p. viii.)

Much of accepted opinion about primitive peoples was seen to be wrong or one-sided in the light of this new information, and, as I mentioned in an earlier lecture, the new information was sufficient in bulk and quality for Morgan, McLennan, Tylor, and others to build out of it a self-contained discipline devoting itself primarily to the study of primitive societies. There was at last a sufficient body of knowledge for speculations to be tested and for new hypotheses to be put forward on a solid basis of ethnographic fact.

When it is said that in the end it is the facts which have decided the fate of theories it must be added that it is not the bare facts but a demonstration of their distribution and significance. Allow me to give you an instance. The matrilineal mode of tracing descent had been recorded for a number of primitive societies by ancient and mediaeval historians, for example, Herodotus for the Lycians and Maqrizi for the Beja, and also by modern observers; Lafitau for the North American Redskins, Bowdich for the Ashanti of the Gold Coast, Grey for the Australian Blackfellows, and other travellers for other peoples;[1] but these records were passed over as mere curiosities till Bachofen and McLennan drew attention to their great importance for sociological theory. Had the material been brought together and its importance thereby established before Maine wrote *Ancient Law*, he could hardly have taken the certain line he took in that book and which he was forced to modify in his later writings in the light of this organized evidence.

McLennan is a very instructive example of the relation of a body of knowledge to theories based on it. He was under no illusion about the value of many of his authori-

[1] Joseph François Lafitau, *Moeurs des Sauvages Ameriquains*, 1724; T. H. Bowdich, *Mission from Cape Coast Castle to Ashantee*, 1819; George Grey, *Journals of Two Expeditions of Discovery in North-West and Western Australia*, 1841.

ties, whose accounts he criticized as thin and vitiated by every kind of personal prejudice, but had he been more cautious than he was he could hardly have avoided some of the errors which led him into a succession of false constructions. On the evidence at his disposal he had every reason for being satisfied that matriliny prevailed universally among the Australian aborigines. We now know that this is not the case. It is also not the case, as he thought, that matriliny prevails among the great majority of existing rude races. He also thought that polyandry had the widest possible distribution, whereas in fact its distribution is very limited. He was also wrong in supposing that female infanticide is widely prevalent among primitive peoples.

The most serious error into which McLennan's authorities led him was to suppose that among the most primitive peoples the institutions of marriage and the family are not found or exist only in a very rudimentary form. Had he known, as we now know, that they are found without exception in all primitive societies he could not have reached the conclusions he arrived at, for they depend absolutely on the dogma that neither marriage nor the family exist in early society, a belief not dispelled till quite recently when Westermarck, and after him Malinowski, showed it to be insupportable in fact.[1]

It could be shown with equal facility that most of the theories of other writers of the time were wrong or inadequate on account of the inaccuracy or insufficiency of the observations then recorded. But even where they went most astray these writers at least put forward hypotheses about primitive societies which provided lines of inquiry for those whose vocations and duties necessitated residence, often very lengthy residence, among

[1] Edward A. Westermarck, *The History of Human Marriage*, 1891; B. Malinowski, *The Family among the Australian Aborigines—A Sociological Study*, 1913.

simple peoples; and we get from this time onwards an exchange between scholars at home and a few missionaries and administrators living in backward parts of the world. These missionaries and administrators were anxious both to make contributions to knowledge and to make use of what anthropology could teach them in seeking to understand their wards. They were made aware by their reading of the literature of anthropology that even those peoples lowest in the scale of material culture have complex social systems, moral codes, religion, art, philosophy, and the rudiments of science, which must be respected and, once understood, can be admired.

The influence of anthropological theories of the time is very evident, sometimes for the better, sometimes for the worse, in the accounts they wrote. Not only were they acquainted with theoretical problems being discussed by scholars, but they were often directly in touch with those who propounded them. It became customary for those at home who wanted information to send out lists of questions to those living among primitive peoples. The first of these was that drawn up by Morgan to elicit kinship terminologies, and sent by him to American agents in foreign countries. It was on the basis of their replies that he published in 1871 his famous *Systems of Consanguinity and Affinity of the Human Family*. Later Sir James Frazer drew up a list of questions, *Questions on the Manners, Customs, Religion, Superstitions, etc., of Uncivilized or Semi-Civilized Peoples*,[1] and sent it to people all over the world in order to obtain information which went into one or other volume of *The Golden Bough*. The most comprehensive of these questionnaires was *Notes and Queries in Anthropology*, first published for the Royal Anthropological Institute in 1874 and now in its fifth edition.

Scholars at home sometimes corresponded regularly with those brought into touch with them through their

[1] No date. Probably in the 'eighties.

writings, for example, Morgan with Fison and Howitt in Australia, and Frazer with Spencer in Australia and Roscoe in Africa, In much more recent times administrative officers have taken courses of anthropology in British universities, a development I speak of more fully in my last lecture. Throughout, a most important link between the scholar at home and the administrator or missionary abroad has been the Royal Anthropological Institute which has since 1843, when it was founded as the Ethnological Society of London, provided a common meeting-place for all interested in the study of primitive man.

Many accounts written about primitive peoples by laymen were excellent, and in a few cases their descriptions have hardly been excelled by the best professional fieldworkers. They were written by men with lengthy experience of the peoples, and who spoke their languages. I refer to such books as Callaway's *The Religious System of the Amazulu* (1870), Codrington's *The Melanesians* (1891), the works of Spencer and Gillen on the Aborigines of Australia,[1] Junod's *The Life of a South African Tribe* (1912–13, French edition, 1898), and Smith and Dale's *The Ila-Speaking Peoples of Northern Rhodesia* (1920). Just as the observations of travellers continued to provide valuable information throughout this period when detailed monographs on primitive peoples were being written by missionaries and administrators, so these detailed studies by laymen continued to have great value for anthropology long after professional fieldwork had become customary.

Nevertheless it became apparent that if the study of social anthropology was to advance, anthropologists would have to make their own observations. It is indeed surprising that, with the exception of Morgan's study of

[1] B. Spencer and F. J. Gillen, *The Native Tribes of Central Australia*, 1899; *The Northern Tribes of Central Australia*, 1904; *The Arunta*, 1927.

the Iroquois,[1] not a single anthropologist conducted field studies till the end of the nineteenth century. It is even more remarkable that it does not seem to have occurred to them that a writer on anthropological topics might at least have a look, if only a glimpse, at one or two specimens of what he spent his life writing about. William James tells us that when he asked Sir James Frazer about natives he had known, Frazer exclaimed, 'But Heaven forbid!'[2]

Had a natural scientist been asked a similar question about the objects of his study he would have replied very differently. As we have noted, Maine, McLennan, Bachofen, and Morgan among the earlier anthropological writers were lawyers. Fustel de Coulanges was a classical and mediaeval historian, Spencer was a philosopher, Tylor was a foreign languages clerk, Pitt-Rivers was a soldier, Lubbock was a banker, Robertson Smith was a Presbyterian minister and a biblical scholar, and Frazer was a classical scholar. The men who now came into the subject were for the most part natural scientists. Boas was a physicist and geographer, Haddon a marine zoologist, Rivers a physiologist, Seligman a pathologist, Elliot Smith an anatomist, Balfour a zoologist, Malinowski a physicist, and Radcliffe-Brown, though he had taken the Moral Sciences Tripos at Cambridge, had also been trained in experimental psychology. These men had been taught that in science one tests hypotheses by one's own observations. One does not rely on laymen to do it for one.

Anthropological expeditions began in America with the work of Boas in Baffin Land and British Columbia, and were initiated in England shortly afterwards by Haddon of Cambridge, who led a band of scholars to

[1] *The League of the Iroquois,* 1851.
[2] Ruth Benedict, 'Anthropology and the Humanities', *American Anthropologist,* 1948, p. 587.

conduct research in the Torres Straits region of the Pacific in 1898 and 1899. This expedition marked a turning-point in the history of social anthropology in Great Britain. From this time two important and inter-connected developments began to take place: anthropology became more and more a whole-time professional study, and some field experience came to be regarded as an essential part of the training of its students.

This early professional fieldwork had many weaknesses. However well the men who carried it out might have been trained in systematic research in one or other of the natural sciences, the short time they spent among the peoples they studied, their ignorance of their languages, and the casualness and superficiality of their contacts with the natives did not permit deep investigation. It is indeed a measure of the advance of anthropology that these early studies appear today to be quite inadequate. Later studies of primitive societies became increasingly more intensive and illuminating. The most important of these was, I think, that of Professor Radcliffe-Brown, a pupil of Rivers and Haddon. His study of the Andaman Islanders from 1906 to 1908[1] was the first attempt by a social anthropologist to investigate sociological theories in a primitive society and to describe the social life of a people in such a way as to bring out clearly what was significant in it for those theories. In this respect it has perhaps greater importance in the history of social anthropology than the Torres Straits expedition, the members of which were interested in ethnological and psychological problems rather than in sociological ones.

We have noted how theoretical speculation about social institutions was at first only incidentally related to descriptive accounts of primitive peoples, and how later social anthropology may be said to have begun when in

[1] A. R. Brown, *The Andaman Islanders—A Study in Social Anthropology*, 1922.

the nineteenth century these peoples became the chief field of research for some students of institutions. But the research was entirely literary and based on the observations of others. We have now reached the final, and natural, stage of development, in which observations and the evaluation of them are made by the same person and the scholar is brought into direct contact with the subject of his study. Formerly the anthropologist, like the historian, regarded documents as the raw material of his study. Now the raw material was social life itself.

Bronislaw Malinowski, a pupil of Hobhouse, Westermarck, and Seligman, carried field research a step further. If Professor Radcliffe-Brown has always had a wider knowledge of general social anthropology and has proved himself the abler thinker, Malinowski was the more thorough fieldworker. He not only spent a longer period than any anthropologist before him, and I think after him also, in a single study of a primitive people, the Trobriand Islanders of Melanesia between 1914 and 1918, but he was also the first anthropologist to conduct his research through the native language, as he was the first to live throughout his work in the centre of native life. In these favourable circumstances Malinowski came to know the Trobriand Islanders well, and he was describing their social life in a number of bulky, and some shorter, monographs up to the time of his death.[1]

Malinowski began lecturing in London in 1924. Professor Firth, now in Malinowski's chair in London, and I were his first two anthropological pupils in that year, and between 1924 and 1930 most of the other social anthropologists who now hold chairs in Great Britain and the Dominions were taught by him. It can be fairly said that the comprehensive field studies of modern anthropology directly or indirectly derive from

[1] *Argonauts of the Western Pacific*, 1922; *The Sexual Life of Savages*, 1929; *Coral Gardens and their Magic*, 1935.

his teaching, for he insisted that the social life of a
primitive people can only be understood if it is studied
intensively, and that it is a necessary part of a social
anthropologist's training to carry out at least one such
intensive study of a primitive society. I shall discuss what
this means when I have drawn your attention in a few
words to what I think is an important feature of the
earlier field studies by professional anthropologists.

These studies were carried out among very small-scale
political communities—Australian hordes, Andamanese
camps, and Melanesian villages—and this circumstance
had the effect that certain aspects of social life, particularly kinship and ritual, were inquired into to the neglect
of others, especially of political structure, which was not
given the attention it deserved till African societies began
to be studied. In Africa autonomous political groups
often number many thousands of members, and their
internal political organization as well as their interrelations forced the attention of students to specifically
political problems. This is a very recent development,
for professional research in Africa was not opened till the
visit of Professor and Mrs. Seligman to the Anglo-
Egyptian Sudan in 1909–1910, and the first intensive
study in Africa by a social anthropologist was that carried
out by myself among the Azande of the Anglo-Egyptian
Sudan, starting in 1927. Since then, most intensive
studies of primitive peoples have been made in Africa,
and political institutions have received the attention they
require, as, for example, in Professor Schapera's account
of the Bechuana, Professor Fortes's account of the
Tallensi of the Gold Coast, Professor Nadel's account of
the Nupe of Nigeria, Dr. Kuper's account of the Swazi,
and my own account of the Nuer of the Anglo-Egyptian
Sudan.

I will now tell you, so that you may understand better
what is meant by intensive fieldwork, what is today

required of a person who wishes to become a professional social anthropologist. I speak particularly of our arrangements at Oxford. There a man comes to us with a degree in another subject, and he first spends a year working for the Diploma in Anthropology, a course which gives him a general knowledge of social anthropology, and also, as I explained in my first lecture, some acquaintance with physical anthropology, ethnology, technology, and prehistoric archaeology. He spends a second year, and perhaps longer, in writing a thesis from the literature of social anthropology for the degree of B.Litt. or B.Sc. Then, if his work has been of sufficient merit and if he is lucky, he obtains a grant for field research and prepares himself for it by a careful study of the literature on the peoples of the region in which he is to conduct it, including their languages.

He then usually spends at least two years in a first field study of a primitive society, this period covering two expeditions and a break between them for collating the material collected on the first expedition. Experience has shown that a few months' break, preferably spent in a university department, is essential for sound fieldwork. It will take him at least another five years to publish the results of his research to the standards of modern scholarship, and much longer should he have other calls on his time; so that it can be reckoned that an intensive study of a single primitive society and the publication of its results take about ten years.

A study of a second society is desirable, because otherwise an anthropologist is likely to think for the rest of his life, as Malinowski did, in terms of one particular type of society. This second study usually takes a shorter time because the anthropologist has learnt from his previous experience to conduct research quickly and to write with economy, but it will certainly be several years before his researches are published. To stay this long course of training and research demands great patience.

In this sketch of an anthropologist's training, I have only told you that he must make intensive studies of primitive peoples. I have not yet told you how he makes them. How does one make a study of a primitive people? I will answer this question very briefly and in very general terms, stating only what we regard as the essential rules of good fieldwork and omitting any discussion of special techniques of inquiry. What special techniques we have are in any case very simple and amount to little; and some of them, like questionnaires and censuses, cannot fruitfully be employed unless the people being studied have reached a higher degree of sophistication than is found among simple peoples before their traditional way of life has been much altered by trade, education and administration. There is indeed much to be said for Radin's contention that 'most good investigators are hardly aware of the precise manner in which they gather their data.'[1]

Nevertheless, experience has proved that certain conditions are essential if a good investigation is to be carried out. The anthropologist must spend sufficient time on the study, he must throughout be in close contact with the people among whom he is working, he must communicate with them solely through their own language, and he must study their entire culture and social life. I will examine each of these desiderata for, obvious though they may be, they are the distinguishing marks of British anthropological research which make it, in my opinion, different from and of a higher quality than research conducted elsewhere.

The earlier professional fieldworkers were always in a great hurry. Their quick visits to native peoples sometimes lasted only a few days, and seldom more than a

[1] Paul Radin, *The Method and Theory of Ethnology*, 1933, p. ix.

77

few weeks. Survey research of this kind can be a useful preliminary to intensive studies and elementary ethnological classifications can be derived from it, but it is of little value for an understanding of social life. The position is very different today when, as I have said, one to three years are devoted to the study of a single people. This permits observations to be made at every season of the year, the social life of the people to be recorded to the last detail, and conclusions to be tested systematically.

However, even given unlimited time for his research, the anthropologist will not produce a good account of the people he is studying unless he can put himself in a position which enables him to establish ties of intimacy with them, and to observe their daily activities from within, and not from without, their community life. He must live as far as possible in their villages and camps, where he is, again as far as possible, physically and morally part of the community. He then not only sees and hears what goes on in the normal everyday life of the people as well as less common events, such as ceremonies and legal cases, but by taking part in those activities in which he can appropriately engage, he learns through action as well as by ear and eye what goes on around him. This is very unlike the situation in which records of native life were compiled by earlier anthropological fieldworkers, and also by missionaries and administrators, who, living out of the native community in mission stations or government posts, had mostly to rely on what a few informants told them. If they visited native villages at all, their visits interrupted and changed the activities they had come to observe.

This is not merely a matter of physical proximity. There is also a psychological side to it. By living among the natives as far as he can like one of themselves the anthropologist puts himself on a level with them. Unlike the administrator and missionary he has no authority and status to maintain, and unlike them he has a neutral position. He is not there to change their way of life but as a humble learner of it; and he has no retainers and intermediaries who obtrude between him and the people, no police, interpreters, or catechists to screen him off from them.

What is perhaps even more important for his work is the fact that he is all alone, cut off from the companionship of men of his own race and culture, and is dependent on the natives around him for company, friendship, and human understanding. An anthropologist has failed unless, when he says goodbye to the natives, there is on both sides the sorrow of parting. It is evident that he can only establish this intimacy if he makes himself in some degree a member of their society and lives, thinks, and feels in their culture since only he, and not they, can make the necessary transference.

It is obvious that if the anthropologist is to carry out his work in the conditions I have described he must learn the native language, and any anthropologist worth his salt will make the learning of it his first task and will altogether, even at the beginning of his study, dispense with interpreters. Some do not pick up strange languages easily, and many primitive languages are almost unbelievably difficult to learn, but the language must be mastered as thoroughly as the capacity of the student and its complexities permit, not only because the anthropologist can then communicate freely with the natives, but for further reasons. To understand a people's thought one has to think in their symbols. Also, in learning the language one learns the culture and the social system which are conceptualized in the language. Every kind of social relationship, every belief, every technological process—in fact everything in the social life of the natives—is expressed in words as well as in action, and when one has fully understood the meaning of all the words of their language in all their situations of reference one has finished one's study of the society. I may add that, as every experienced fieldworker knows, the most difficult task in anthropological fieldwork is to determine the meanings of a few key words, upon an understanding of which the success of the whole investigation depends; and they can only be determined by the anthropologist himself learning to use the words correctly in his converse with the natives. A further reason for learning the native language at the beginning of the investigation is that it places the anthropologist in a position of complete dependence on the natives. He comes to them as pupil, not as master.

Finally, the anthropologist must study the whole of the social life. It is impossible to understand clearly and comprehensively any part of a people's social life except in the full context of their social life as a whole. Though he may not publish every detail he has recorded, you will find in a good anthropologist's notebooks a detailed description of even the most commonplace activities, for example, how a cow is milked or how meat is cooked. Also, though he may decide to write a book on a people's law, on their religion, or on their economics, describing one aspect of their life and neglecting the rest, he does so always against the background of their entire social activities and in terms of their whole social structure.

Such, very briefly and roughly, are the essential conditions of good anthropological fieldwork. We may now ask what are the qualifications required for it. Obviously, in the first place the fieldworker must have had an academic training in social anthropology. He must have a good knowledge both of general theory and of the ethnography of the region in which he is to work.

It is true that any educated, intelligent and sensitive person can get to know a strange people well and write an excellent account of their way of life, and I would say that he often gets to know them better and writes a better book about them than many professional anthropologists do. Many excellent ethnographic accounts were written long before social anthropology was even heard of, for example Dubois's *Hindu Manners, Customs and Ceremonies* (1816) and Lane's *An Account of the Manners and Customs of the Modern Egyptians* (1836). This cannot be denied, but I think that it is also certainly true that, even on the level of translation from one culture into another, without taking structural analysis into account, a man who in addition to his other qualifications has been trained in social anthropology will make a much deeper and fuller study, for one has to learn what to look for and how to observe.

When we come to the stage of structural analysis the layman is lost, because here a knowledge of theory, of problems, of method, and of technical concepts is essential. I can go for a walk and come back and give you an account of the rocks I have seen. It may be an excellent description, but it will not be a geological one. Likewise, a layman can give an account of the social life of a primitive people but, however descriptively excellent, it will not be a sociological account. The difference here is, of course, that in the geologist's study of rocks only scientific knowledge and technical skills and tools are required, whereas in the anthropological study of peoples all sorts of personal and human qualities are involved which the layman may possess and the anthropologist lack. It is possible to put oneself in the position of a man of alien culture, but not of a rock.

Anthropological fieldwork therefore requires in addition to theoretical knowledge and technical training a certain kind of character and temperament. Some men cannot stand the strain of isolation, especially in what are often uncomfortable and unhealthy conditions. Others cannot make the intellectual and emotional transference required. The native society has to be in the anthropologist himself and not merely in his notebooks if he is to understand it, and the capacity to think and feel alternately as a savage and as a European is not easily acquired, if indeed it can be acquired at all.

To succeed in this feat a man must be able to abandon himself without reserve, and he must also have intuitive powers which not all possess. Most people who know what and how to observe can make a merely competent study of a primitive people, but when one has to estimate whether a man will make a study which will be on a deeper level of understanding one looks for more than intellectual ability and technical training, for these qualities will not in themselves make a good anthropologist any more than they will make a good historian. What comes out of a study of a primitive people derives not merely from intellectual impressions of native life but from its impact on the entire personality, on the observer as a total human being. It follows that successful fieldwork may in some degree depend on the suitability of a particular man for the study of a particular people. A man who might fail in the study of one people might succeed in the study of another people. If he is to succeed, his interest and sympathy must be aroused.

If the right kind of temperament is not always found with ability, special training, and love of careful scholarship, it is rarely combined also with the imaginative insight of the artist which is required in interpretation of what is observed, and the literary skill necessary to translate a foreign culture into the language of one's own. The work of the anthropologist is not photographic. He has to decide what is significant in what he observes and by his subsequent relation of his experiences to bring what is significant into relief. For this he must have, in addition to a wide knowledge of anthropology, a feeling for form and pattern, and a touch of genius. I am not suggesting that any of us have all the qualities which make the perfect fieldworker. Some are gifted in one way and some in another, and each uses as best he can what talents he has.

Since in anthropological fieldwork much must depend, as I think we would all admit, on the person who conducts it, it may well be asked whether the same results would have been obtained had another person made a particular investigation. This is a very difficult question. My own answer would be, and I think that the evidence we have on the matter shows it to be a correct one, that the bare record of fact would be much the same, though there would, of course, be some individual differences even at the level of perception.

It is almost impossible for a person who knows what he is looking for, and how to look for it, to be mistaken about the facts if he spends two years among a small and culturally homogeneous people doing nothing else but studying their way of life. He gets to know so well what will be said and done in any situation—the social life becomes so familiar to him—that there ceases to be much point in his making any further observations or in asking any further questions, Also, whatever kind of person he may be, the anthropologist is working within a body of theoretical knowledge which largely determines his interests and his lines of inquiry. He is also working within the limits imposed by the culture of the people he is studying. If they are pastoral nomads he must study pastoral nomadism. If they are obsessed by witchcraft, he must study witchcraft. He has no choice but to follow the cultural grain.

But while I think that different social anthropologists who studied the same people would record much the same facts in their notebooks, I believe that they would write different kinds of books. Within the limits imposed by their discipline and the culture under investigation

anthropologists are guided in choice of themes, in selection and arrangement of facts to illustrate them, and in
judgment of what is and what is not significant, by their
different interests, reflecting differences of personality,
of education, of social status, of political views, of religious convictions, and so forth.

One can only interpret what one sees in terms of one's
own experience and of what one is, and anthropologists,
while they have a body of knowledge in common, differ
in other respects as widely as other people in their back-
grounds of experience and in themselves. The personality
of an anthropologist cannot be eliminated from his work
any more than the personality of an historian can be
eliminated from his. Fundamentally, in his account of a
primitive people the anthropologist is not only describing
their social life as accurately as he can but is expressing
himself also. In this sense his account must express moral
judgment, especially where it touches matters on which
he feels strongly; and what comes out of a study will to
this extent at least depend on what the individual brings
to it. Those who know anthropologists and their writings
as well as I do, would, I think, accept this conclusion.
If allowances are made for the personality of the writer,
and if we consider that in the entire range of anthropological studies the effects of these personal differences
tend to correct each other, I do not think that we need
worry unduly over this problem in so far as the reliability
of anthropological findings is in question.

There is a broader aspect to the question. However
much anthropologists may differ among themselves they
are all children of the same culture and society. In the
main they all have, apart from their common specialist
knowledge and training, the same cultural categories and
values which direct their attention to selected characteristics of the societies being studied. Religion, law,
economics, politics, and so forth, are abstract categories

of our culture into which observations on the life of primitive peoples are patterned. Certain kinds of fact are noticed, and they are seen in a certain kind of way, by people of our culture. To some extent at any rate, people who belong to different cultures would notice different facts and perceive them in a different way. In so far as this is true, the facts recorded in our notebooks are not social facts but ethnographic facts, selection and interpretation having taken place at the level of observation. I cannot now discuss, but only state, this general question of perception and evaluation.

I must say in conclusion that, as you will have noted, I have been discussing anthropological field research and the qualities and qualifications required for it in the light of the opinion I expressed in my last lecture that social anthropology is best regarded as an art and not as a natural science. Those among my colleagues who hold the opposite opinion might have discussed the questions with which I have been concerned in this lecture in a rather different way.

V

MODERN ANTHROPOLOGICAL STUDIES

I endeavoured in my second and third lectures to give you some account of the theoretical development of social anthropology, which has meant more or less in practice the development of theories about primitive societies or what in the last century would have been called the institutions of early man, and in the century before, rude society. In my last lecture I briefly reviewed the growth of our knowledge about these primitive societies, and I explained how descriptive accounts of them had improved, both in quality and in quantity, from the casual observations of explorers, through the detailed records of missionaries and administrators, to the intensive studies of modern professional research. The theories have been shaped and reshaped by this steady growth in knowledge and they have on their side, in each reformulation, directed observation into deeper layers and into new fields of the social life of primitive peoples and thereby led to further increase in knowledge.

The great development in research has produced a new orientation in the aims and methods of social anthropology. I will give you in this lecture a brief account of some of the tendencies it has given rise to, and I will then discuss a few anthropological monographs, in which fieldworkers have recorded and arranged their observations, as examples of the kind of inquiry in which social anthropologists now engage. We have seen how they make their observations. We will now examine how they organize them and the use to which they put them.

The essential point to remember is that the anthropologist is working within a body of theoretical knowledge and that he makes his observations to solve problems which derive from it. This emphasis on problems is, of course, a feature of any field of scholarship. Lord Acton told his history students to study problems and not periods. Collingwood told his archaeological students to study problems and not sites. We tell our anthropological students to study problems and not peoples.

The earlier fieldwork monographs were for the most part descriptive accounts of one or other people without much attempt at systematic analysis, though pseudo-historical speculations were sometimes taken for such. Each study consisted of a succession of chapters treating seriatim and in detail a different aspect of social life: environment, racial characteristics, demography, vital statistics, technology, economy, social organization, *rites de passage*, law, religion, magic, mythology, folklore, pastimes, etc. Modern fieldwork monographs are generally intended to give more than merely a description of the social life of a people with interpretations of the more popular kind which any description of one culture in terms of another necessarily entails. They aim at an analytical and integrative description which will bring out those features of the social life which are significant for an understanding of its structure and for general theory.

This followed necessarily as soon as the student of theory began to conduct his own field research. It means that the facts, that is, the observations recorded in the anthropologist's notebooks, are not set forth in his publications as a description of what a primitive people do and say, but to show that what they do and say, apart from its intrinsic interest, illuminates some problem of one or other aspect of culture or institutional life. In other words, in deciding what he is to put into his book and what to leave out of it, he is guided by the relevance of the material for a particular theme designed to bring out significant features of some system of social activities.

I had better say here that in this writing-up side of his work the social anthropologist faces a serious difficulty. We have noted that he makes a study of the entire life of a people. Is it his duty to publish a full record of all his observations on every aspect of their life? The historian is not faced here with the same difficulty. He can select from the material at his disposal what is relevant to his theme and neglect the rest. What he leaves out of his books is not lost. The anthropologist, and to a large extent the archaeologist also, are in a very different position, for what they do not record may be, and often is, lost for ever. The anthropologist is not only the collator and interpreter of sources. He is the creator of them.

It has therefore often been held that it is the duty of a fieldworker not only to record, but also to publish, everything he has observed, whether it has any interest for him or not, on the ground that the first task of anthropology at this time is to assemble as large a body of facts as possible while there are still primitive societies to be studied. The anthropologist is recorder, not arbiter. For him to decide that one fact is important and another fact unimportant is to prejudge the interests of future generations. This is a difficulty which we try to meet in various ways. The prevailing practice tends to be for the fieldworker to publish monographs on one or other aspect of the life of a primitive people which seems to him to have particular importance, using for the purpose only such facts as are relevant to his selected themes and are sufficient to illustrate them. The rest are published in learned journals or are recorded in mimeographed or microfilm form.

The enormous mass of information which can be collected during a two years' study of a primitive people makes, even if this solution is adopted, for a change, already very noticeable, in anthropological method. We have seen that in the past anthropologists were devotees of the comparative method. Whether the aim was to reconstruct history or to reach general descriptive formulas the procedure was the same. A great number of books were read and the information bearing on the subject of inquiry was extracted from them and pieced together to make a new book. Without entering again into a consideration of the value of this kind of literary comparative study, it is a matter of plain experience that it is a formidable task which cannot be undertaken by a man who is under the obligation to publish the results of the two or three field studies he has made, since this will take him the rest of his life to complete if he has heavy teaching and administrative duties as well. As almost all social anthropologists do fieldwork today the situation is a general one.

It is evident that in these circumstances social anthropology would soon disintegrate into an endless succession of disconnected studies if there were not a common method of research to take the place of the older use of the comparative method. This is supplied today, as a result of social anthropology having become a field, or observational, study by what would in the natural sciences be called the experimental method. What I mean by this will be clear to you if I take an example.

An anthropologist has made a study of religious cults in some primitive society and has reached certain conclusions about their role in social life. If he formulates these clearly and in terms which allow them to be broken down into problems of research it is then possible for the same, or another, anthropologist to make in a second society observations which will show whether these conclusions have wider validity. He will probably find that some of them hold, that some of them do not hold, and that some hold with modifications. Starting from the point reached by the first study, the second is likely to drive the investigation deeper and to add some new formulations to the confirmed conclusions of the first. We now have a hypothesis about the religious cults of primitive peoples derived from a study of them in two societies. A third study is now made, and then a fourth and a fifth. The process can be continued indefinitely. If the studies are systematic and each is used to test the conclusions reached up to that point and to advance new hypotheses which permit verification, each will reach, as knowledge increases and new problems emerge, a deeper level of investigation which in its turn will lead to a clearer definition of concepts. Every new study, if it is of any value, not only tells us about a certain institution in the particular primitive society studied, but sheds light on significant features of that institution in other societies, including those in which the importance of these features may not have been realized by earlier investigators. Field research of today is in this sense experimental. It is also, in a rather different sense, comparative; but it is very unlike what used to be called the comparative method, which has largely been abandoned, partly for the reason I have given and partly because it seldom provides answers to the questions asked.

A further change of direction follows from what I have been saying. Not only the method but to some extent the aim of research has changed. It stands to reason that field research is incompatible with those schemes of social development favoured by nineteenth-century anthropologists. One cannot observe events which have long passed and of which no memory has been preserved. In a field study of a primitive people there is no means one can use to prove or disprove the hypothesis that they were once matrilineal or lived in a state of sexual promiscuity.

Apart from this, the scope of inquiry is inevitably narrowed into small problems within the limits of which inquiry is possible and may lead to fruitful conclusions. Ambitious efforts at world-wide synthesis give way to humbler and less spectacular inquiries. Whereas the nineteenth-century anthropologist sought to answer such questions as 'What is the sociological significance of religion?', no anthropologist, or at any rate no sensible anthropologist, would ask such a question today. Rather he seeks to determine, for instance, the part played by the ancestor cult in a social system of the type we call a segmentary lineage system among certain African peoples. Instead of attempting to paint on a grand canvas the development of the notion of responsibility, or the development of the state, in the whole human race, the anthropologist of today concentrates on such small problems as can be investigated by direct inquiry and observation, such as the function of the feud, or the position of chieftainship of a certain kind, in societies where the social activities centred around these institutions can be seen and studied. Instead of discussing whether primitive societies are communistic or individualistic the anthropologist of today makes a detailed study of the complex of rights, some corporate and some personal, centred in property, maybe in land or in cattle, in a particular society to discover how these rights are related to one another and to the social systems in which they figure, kinship systems, political systems, systems of cult, and so forth.

The viewpoint in social anthropology today may be summed up by saying that we now think we can learn more about the nature of human society by really detailed intensive and observational studies, conducted in a series of a few selected societies with the aim of solving limited problems, than by attempting generalizations on a wider scale from literature. As a result we are just beginning to know a little bit about the social life of primitive peoples.

The emphasis placed by modern social anthropology on intensive fieldwork studies in which limited problems are tackled has had a further consequence to which I would like to draw your attention before giving you some examples of modern studies. I have remarked in earlier lectures that the nineteenth-century anthropologists were cultural realists. They were interested in customs, and customs were to them independent entities. They were things one society had and another society did not have. Even so sociologically minded a writer as McLennan regarded exogamy, totemism, matriliny, and so forth as items of custom, which, added up, made cultures. Consequently a people either had rules of exogamy or they did not have them; they were either totemistic or they were not; they were either patrilineal or matrilineal.

This kind of cultural taxonomy is slowly being discarded by English social anthropologists. Much could be said on this subject, but it must suffice to say that the modern anthropologist tends to think more in terms of society than of culture—of social systems and values and their interrelations. He asks not so much whether people have rules of exogamy but, for example, what is the significance of these rules for the study of their intercommunity relations. He is not content to know that people have totemic beliefs but seeks to discover how these beliefs may reflect values of descent and the solidarity of groups based on descent. He does not consider that to know that people trace descent through women, and not through men, is significant knowledge in itself. He investigates rather, again for example, how their matrilineal mode of tracing descent affects the brother-sister relationship or the mother's brother-sister's son relationship. Some of these modern studies, as you will see shortly, are more abstract and structural than others—there is a good deal of divergence of opinion about methods of analysis—but they all tend to be, compared with earlier studies, sociological and functional. I now give you some illustrations.

I start with the summary of one of Malinowski's books because he was the first professional anthropologist to do intensive fieldwork through the native language. Although he collected a vast amount of material about the Trobriand Islanders and published several volumes on them before his death, he gave only a partial account of this people, and we are still in the dark about some of their most important activities, particularly about their political organization and their kinship system. The book I am going to discuss, *Argonauts of the Western Pacific* (1922), though long-winded and written in a journalistic style, may be regarded none the less, and not only because of its priority but on its merits, as a classic of descriptive ethnography.

The book is about one set of activities of the Trobriand Islanders which they call *kula*. They and the inhabitants of some neighbouring islands form a kind of league for the exchange of certain objects, long necklaces of red shell and bracelets of white shell. In the system of exchange the necklaces pass through communities one way round the circuit of islands, and the bracelets pass the opposite way round. These objects have no practical value but only a ritual and prestige value, the prestige consisting in the renown a man gets by receiving, possessing, and then passing on particularly esteemed objects. Those men who take part in these exchanges have partners in the islands they visit. The exchanges take place with formality and decorum, and there must be no haggling; though when the ritual exchanges are completed ordinary commercial transactions, bargaining for food or articles of practical use, takes place. The *kula* proper, however, is the system of ritual exchange within which the necklaces and bracelets go round the island communities in everlasting circuit.

To carry out these exchanges the chiefs of villages and groups of nearby villages organize large trading expeditions. This means the preparation of canoes, nautical knowledge, knowledge of magical spells to aid against the chances of the adventure, and knowledge of tradition and myth to guide the Argonauts in their voyages and negotiations. Therefore Malinowski felt that he had to give in the compass of a single book an account of all these, and many other, matters. He had to give us detailed accounts of magic and myth, to describe the scenery for us, to tell us how the natives cultivate their gardens, what is the social position of their women, how they construct and sail their canoes, and so on—even what went on inside himself as well, for he was there too. He paints a picture of the living reality of Trobriand society which brings to the mind the novels of Emile Zola.

We see very clearly in this his first, and I think his best, book on the Trobriand Islanders his conception of what constitutes a social system and a functional analysis of it. To him a social system is a succession of activities or events, and not a set of abstractions. To go on an expedition, Trobriand Islanders make canoes. In making canoes, they utter magical spells. These spells have stories, or myths, accounting for their origin. They also belong to someone by inheritance from his maternal uncle. In the making of a canoe and in planning the expedition there is organization of labour and direction by the chiefs. The chiefs have authority largely because they are richer than commoners. They are richer because they have bigger gardens. They have bigger gardens because they have several wives. To Malinowski all these different activities form a system because each is dependent on all the others and the function of each is the part it plays in the total set of activities which have a direct or indirect bearing on the exchange of the ritual objects of the *kula*.

It is true that in a sense they do form a system of activities, and this mode of impressionistic presentation of social life is very effective, but, properly speaking, the theme is no more than a descriptive synthesis of events. It is not a theoretical integration, though theoretical problems are discussed in interludes in the course of the story. There is consequently no real standard of relevance, since everything has a time and space relationship in cultural reality to everything else, and from whatever point one starts one spreads oneself over the same ground. A description of social life in terms of various aspects of it on this level of events leads inevitably to endless repetitions and to so-called theoretical conclusions which are no more than redescriptions in more abstract language, since discrete correlations can hardly be perceived if one does not depart from concrete reality. Malinowski might have started from chieftainship and described the *kula* in relation to that institution, or he might have written his book on magic and described the *kula* and chieftainship in relation to that.

It is because he seldom made abstractions that Malinowski failed to see clearly what is perhaps the most significant feature of the *kula*, the bringing together, through the acceptance of common ritual values, of politically autonomous communities. Also, comparison between the social life of a people so described and the social life of other peoples similarly portrayed is limited to assessment of cultural similarities and divergences and cannot be of a structural kind, for which abstraction is required. Nevertheless, some excellent and important ethnographic studies of a number of primitive peoples made on what is still very largely the level of cultural realism by students of Malinowski have enriched the literature of our subject: for example, Professor Firth's *We, the Tikopia* (1936), Miss Hunter's *Reaction to Conquest* (1936), Professor Schapera's *A Handbook of Tswana Law and Custom* (1938), and Dr. Richards's *Land, Labour and Diet in Northern Rhodesia* (1939).

Abstraction can mean several different things. It can mean treating only a part of social life for particular and limited problems of investigation, taking the rest into consideration only in so far as it is relevant to these problems, or it can mean structural analysis through the integration of abstractions from social life. As an example of the first procedure I will discuss Dr. Mead's *Coming of Age in Samoa* (1929). This is a discursive, or perhaps I should say chatty and feminine, book with a leaning towards the picturesque, what I call the rustling-of-the-wind-in-the-palm-trees kind of anthropological writing, for which Malinowski set the fashion.

The aim of the book is to show that the difficulties of adolescence, particularly those of adolescent girls, which are so common and troublesome a feature of American life, do not occur in Samoa and may therefore be regarded as a product of a particular type of social environment, as due to the restraints of civilization and not to nature. Dr. Mead therefore sets out to show us in what way Samoan conditions of adolescence are different from those of American adolescence. With this end in view she tells us everything she observed about the social setting of the Samoan girl, how, in a broad sense, she is educated, what her childhood is like, and about her place in the life of the household, village, and wider community, and her variety of sexual relations with young men. The description is always with particular reference to the problem of the investigation, the moulding of the personality of the growing girl by social conditions and the reactions of this personality to the physiological changes of puberty.

The conclusion of the study is that there are no differences between American girls and Samoan girls in the process of adolescence itself. The differences lie in the response to it. In Samoa there is no stress or crisis but an orderly development of interests and activities. 'The girls' minds', Dr. Mead tells us, 'were perplexed by no conflicts, troubled by no philosophical queries, beset by no remote ambitions. To live as a girl with many lovers as long as possible and then to marry in one's own village, near one's own relatives and to have many children, these were uniform and satisfying ambitions.'[1]

The American girl at the same time of her life suffers from strains and stresses because her social environment is different. What are the significant differences? Dr. Mead is of the opinion that the most important are to be found in the absence in Samoa of deep personal feelings and of conflicting values. The Samoan girls do not care very deeply about anyone or anything, and in particular they do not set high hopes on any one relationship. This is partly due to the fact that they are not brought up in a narrow family circle but in a wider circle of kin, so that both authority and affection are spread over a large number of persons. Even more important is the homogeneous culture of the Samoans. They all have the same standards of behaviour. There is only one set of religious beliefs and there is only one code of morals. Consequently in these matters Samoan adolescents do not have to make choices, inevitably affecting their relationships with those around them, and they therefore avoid the conflicts which follow from having to choose between different sets of values and the maladjustments and neuroses which result from the conflicts. The American adolescent, on the contrary, is confronted in her social environment with

[1] P. 157.

so many various and conflicting values that she has to make a choice, and choice is the forerunner of conflict.

The book I have just discussed differs from most modern field monographs in that no analysis of Samoan social structure is presented, even in outline, so that it is difficult to see the facts related in any sort of perspective. Nevertheless, it is a good example of the single-problem kind of study, and it is written by a highly intelligent woman.

I am now going to give you the argument in two books of my own. I must apologize for doing so, but it is easier to present an analysis within a culture that is familiar to one than in an unfamiliar culture. These two books illustrate the use of abstraction of a rather different kind. The first is a study of a system of ideas and the second a study of a system of political groups.

My first book, *Witchcraft, Oracles and Magic among the Azande* (1937), is about a Central African people. It is an attempt to make intelligible a number of beliefs, all of which are foreign to the mentality of a modern Englishman, by showing how they form a comprehensible system of thought, and how this system of thought is related to social activities, social structure, and the life of the individual.

Among the Azande any misfortune can be, and generally is, attributed to witchcraft, which the Azande consider to be an internal organic condition, though its action is believed to be psychic. The witch despatches what they call the soul, or spirit, of his witchcraft to cause damage to others. The sufferer consults oracles, of which the Azande have a number of different kinds, or a diviner, to discover who is injuring him. This may be quite a complicated and lengthy procedure. When the culprit is revealed he is requested to withdraw his malign influence.

If in a case of sickness he does not do so and the invalid

dies, the kinsmen of the dead man could in the past take the affair to their prince's jurisdiction and exact vengeance or compensation, or they could make, as they invariably do in the circumstances today, lethal magic to destroy the witch. In addition to this lethal magic the Azande have a vast body of magical knowledge and techniques, some requiring membership of special magical associations, which are largely used to protect their persons and activities from witchcraft.

Witchcraft, oracles, and magic thus form a complex system of beliefs and rites which makes sense only when they are seen as interdependent parts of a whole. This system has a logical structure. Granted certain postulates, inferences and action based on them are sound. Witchcraft causes death. Therefore a death is evidence of witchcraft, and the oracles confirm that witchcraft caused it. Magic is made to avenge the death. A neighbour dies soon afterwards and the oracles determine that he died a victim to the magic of vengeance. Each bit of belief fits in with every other bit in a general mosaic of mystical thought. If in such a closed system of thought a belief is contradicted by a particular experience this merely shows that the experience was mistaken, or inadequate, or the contradiction is accounted for by secondary elaborations of belief which provide satisfactory explanations of the apparent inconsistency. Even scepticism supports the beliefs about which it is exercised. Criticism of a particular diviner, for example, or distrust of a particular oracle or form of magic, merely enhances faith in others and the system as a whole.

An analysis of a great number of situations in which discussions about witchcraft arose and of comments on the notion by Azande on many occasions showed further that it provides them with a philosophy of events which is intellectually satisfying. At first sight it looks absurd to hold that if termites have gnawed away the supports of a granary and it falls on a man sitting in the shade beneath and kills him, this is an act of witchcraft; but the Azande do not suppose, any more than we would, that the collapse of the granary is not the immediate cause of death. What they say is that it would not have collapsed at a particular moment when a particular man was sitting under it unless the man had been bewitched. Why should it not have fallen at a different moment or when a different man was sitting under it? It is easy to account for the collapse of the granary. That was due to termites and the weight of millet in it. It is also easy to account for the man being under it. He was there for shade in the heat of the day. But why did these two chains of events coincide at a certain point in space and time? We say that the coincidence was chance. The Azande explain it by witchcraft. Witchcraft and the granary operating together killed the man.

The notion of witchcraft gives the Azande not only a natural philosophy but also a moral philosophy, in which is contained also a theory of psychology. Even if a man is a witch, his witchcraft does not harm people unless there is an act of will. There has to be a motive and this is always to be found in the evil passions of men, in hatred, greed, envy, jealousy, and resentment. Misfortunes spring from witchcraft, and witchcraft is directed by evil intentions. Azande do not blame a man for being a witch. He cannot help that. It is the evil in him which makes him harm others that they denounce. I may add that Azande are well aware of what psychologists call projection, that when a man says that another hates him and is bewitching him it is often the first who is the hater and the witch; and that they also realize the significant part played by dreams, or what is now called the subconscious, in the evil passions of men. It is also necessary to point out that the dogma that it is evil which, through witchcraft, causes misfortune cannot be pleaded as an excuse for actions which are due to vice or ignorance. Witchcraft only causes undeserved misfortunes. A man who commits adultery or is disloyal to his king or who fails in some enterprise, such as pot-making, through lack of skill is responsible for the penalties or failures his actions incur.

Since a witch only injures a man when he is ill-disposed towards him, a sufferer from sickness or other misfortune places the names of his enemies before the oracles, and consequently it is an enemy whom the oracles, declare to be the man bewitching him. Accusations of witchcraft consequently only arise between persons whose social relations with one another permit states of enmity to form. Their incidence is determined by the social structure. For example, the relations between children and adults are not such that enmity is likely to arise between them, so that children are not accused of bewitching adults. For a similar reason nobles are not accused of bewitching commoners, though in this case there is the further reason that no commoner would dare to accuse a noble of witchcraft. Likewise, since in Zande society women do not have social relations with men other than their kin and their husbands—and they would not injure their kin—they are only accused of bewitching their female neighbours or their husbands, and not other men.

The oracles have an order of importance. Some are less certain in their revelations than others and action cannot be taken on their statements till these are confirmed by the highest authority, the poison oracle. The poison oracle in its turn is regarded as having more or less significance according to the social status of its owner. A case may therefore go from one poison oracle to another, as in our country a case may go from one court to another, till a final verdict is given by a king's oracle, beyond which there is no appeal. The legal machinery which operates in cases of witchcraft is thus ultimately in the hands of a king and his representatives, which makes the social action the belief entails one of the main supports of royal authority. The operation of witchcraft beliefs in the social life are also closely connected with the kinship system, particularly through the custom of vengeance, but I have already said enough to show how what at first sight seems no more than an absurd superstition is discovered by anthropological investigation to be the integrative principle of a system of thought and morals and to have an important role in the social structure.

My second book, *The Nuer. A Description of the Modes of Livelihood and Political Institutions of a Nilotic People* (1940), is about a very different kind of people and society and deals with very different kinds of problems. The Nuer are semi-nomadic cattle herdsmen living in marsh and savannah country in the southern Anglo-Egyptian Sudan. They form a congeries of tribes and, since they have no chiefs and no legal institutions, the task which seemed to be of first importance was to discover the principle of their tribal, or political, integration. It was evident that the Nuer, having a very simple material culture, are highly dependent on their environment and it became clear from an examination of their oecology that the pursuit of a pastoral life in difficult conditions made a fairly wide political order necessary if they were to maintain their way of life. This political order is provided by the tribal structure. A study of the different local communities within a Nuer tribe revealed the fact that each is identified politically with a lineage, though most of its members do not belong to this lineage, and that all these lineages are branches of a single clan. Each of the territorial divisions of a tribe is thus co-ordinated with a corresponding branch of this dominant clan so that relations between the parts of a tribe, both their separateness and their unity, are conceptualized and expressed within a framework of values of descent.

Leaving on one side a number of other matters investigated against this general structural background, I will discuss very briefly the Nuer concepts of time as an example of the kind of problem we investigate and the kind of structural analysis we make.

I can only outline the argument, which shows in part how the conceptualization of natural changes as points of reference in time-reckoning is determined by the rhythm of social activities and in part how the points are reflections of structural relations between social groups. The daily tasks of the kraal are the points of reference for each day, and for longer periods than a day the points are the phases of other recurrent activities, such as weeding or the seasonal movements of men and their herds. The passage of time is the succession of activities and their relations to one another. All sorts of interesting conclusions follow. Time has not the same value at one season of the year that it has at another. Also, since the Nuer have, properly speaking, no abstract system of time-reckoning they do not think of time, as we do, as something actual, which passes, can be wasted, can be saved, and so forth; and they do not have to co-ordinate their activities with an abstract passage of time, because their points of reference are the activities themselves. Thus, in a certain month one makes the first fishing dams and forms the first cattle camps, and since one is doing these things it must be that month or thereabouts. One does not make fishing dams because it is November; it is November because one makes fishing dams.

The larger periods of time are almost entirely structural. The events they relate are different for different groups of people so that each group has its own system of time-reckoning in addition to a common system which refers to events of outstanding significance to them all. Also, male Nuer are stratified by age into divisions or sets, a new age-set starting about every ten years. I will not enter into the details of this arrangement but merely say that the time that events happened is often denoted by reference to these divisions. Hence intervals between events are not reckoned in time concepts, as we understand them, but in terms of structural distance, of the social difference between groups of persons. Nuer also reckon history in terms of their genealogies of descent. Now it can be shown that the depth to which descent is traced in any particular situation corresponds to the size of the group of kin concerned, so that here time is a reflection of units of social structure. Events have a position in structure but no exact position in historical time as we understand it. In general it may be said that among the Nuer time is a conceptualization of the social structure and the points of reference in the system of reckoning are projections into the past of actual relations between groups of persons. It co-ordinates relationships rather than events.

Many steps in so short an exposition must be obscure to you. This does not matter, because I am not trying to prove the soundness of the argument but to show you the method of analysis pursued. You will have seen that here again what the method amounts to is to make some part of the social life intelligible by showing how it is integrated with other parts. This can only be done by making abstractions and interrelating them logically.

I mentioned in my first lecture that social anthropology, although it has generally in the past restricted its attention to primitive societies, has not entirely done so, and is not considered by us to be a study of primitive societies but of all human societies. To show you that we also study civilized societies I will take as my final example of anthropological field monographs a book on the peasantry of Southern Ireland, Professor Arensberg's *The Irish Countryman* (1937). It is an excellent example of structural analysis in which the author sets forth simply and concisely the main conclusions reached by an investigation made in County Clare by himself and Professor Kimball.

Southern Ireland is a country of small farms, the greater part of the farming families supporting themselves on from fifteen to thirty acres, living off the land and selling their surplus products for such necessities as flour and tea. The farmers run their farms on the labour of their families, though they receive some help from kinsmen, the network of kinship ties uniting the members of a village and of neighbouring villages having a fundamental role in the organization of Irish country life. The author discusses these and many other topics. I will briefly recount what he says about two of them, marriage and the relations between countryman and townsman.

We are told that 'Marriage is a turning point round which rural life hinges. It is a structural centre.'[1] The smallest farmers have the largest families, and marriage takes place for both sexes at a later age than in any other country for which records are kept. Owing to the small size of the farms a family can usually marry off only one son and one daughter. When the son who is to get the farm marries, his bride brings him a dowry, usually between about £250 and £350—it must be roughly equivalent to the value of the farm, and is therefore a measure of the family's social status. Part of it goes to the husband and his parents, who after the marriage retire from management of the farm, and part is used to help the other sons who, since the farms are not divided

[1] p. 93.

among the children, must either migrate to the towns to earn their living in trade, a profession, or the church, or emigrate. By this means it is possible to maintain family continuity on a farm, blood and land being closely associated, but only at the expense of the other, generally younger, sons. The author shows in this way how marriage, inheritance, social controls, and migration and emigration all form part of the social system of small farms.

The family system of the farm has its counterpart in the local market towns and this, as you will see, accounts for the dying out of the town families. The younger sons of the farmers go to the towns as apprentices and their daughters as wives. A trader lives on country custom, and this is given only to kinsmen. Consequently a shopkeeper or publican marries his son who is to take over from him his shop or pub to a country girl, who will bring with her not only her dowry but also the custom of her part of the countryside. Town and country, the distributive unit and the productive unit, are thus bound together not only economically but through ties of kinship. But urban life affects the outlook of the men, who, bit by bit, can no longer meet the countryman halfway. They lose rural ways and interests, and this is even more so with those born in the towns, the second generation migrants. So the shopkeeper's and publican's families move into professions or into larger towns. They become part of a social milieu in which the countryside has no part, and new blood fills their places in the market town and succeeds by virtue of its country connections, bringing with it new bonds of kinship. We see thus how the economic system, through the exchange of farm products for articles of trade, and the kinship system, through intermarriage between town and country, are bound up together in the general social system of the Irish countryside.

MODERN ANTHROPOLOGICAL STUDIES

One of the ways in which the connection between townsmen and their country cousins is maintained and expressed is by debt. The countryman is always in debt to his shopkeeper kinsman, and this chronic debt is part of their social relationship. Indeed, when a countryman is angry with a shopkeeper he pays his debt to withdraw his custom and sever their relationship. The debt, like the dowry, is a measure of status, being a sign of one's ability and willingness to support that network of social obligations which gives oneself and one's family a place in social life. The debt passes down the generations from father to son. It is the bond between the family and kin of the farmer and the family and kin of the shopkeeper by which they express in each other confidence and social obligation. Debt is thus shown in a new light, as one of the mechanisms by which a social system is maintained. It cannot be understood merely in economic or legal terms but only in relation to kinship and other features of the total social structure; and moral judgment about it has to be made in the light of this broader understanding.

These few examples—all I have time to give—will, I trust, have shown you the type and diversity of problems with which social anthropologists are today concerned. Once again, you will note that they are not inquiries into the strange or romantic but into matter-of-fact problems of sociology, problems which, moreover, as I shall have occasion to emphasize in my next, and final, lecture, are of general importance, and not important merely within their particular ethnic and geographical setting. It is of significance for us in our own society to learn that the Trobriand Islanders expend their greatest energies in pursuit of honour and not of profit; that if the Samoans lack a diversity of ends, and the greater variety of personality these ends engender, they have personal security and the happiness that goes with it; that though modern science rejects the assumptions on which the Zande system of beliefs is based the system has a philosophic and moral validity; that to understand Nuer concepts of time we have first to understand their social structure; and that in Southern Ireland debt serves to uphold harmonious relations between countryman and townsman. These and many other fruitful, if tentative, conclusions have obviously significance for the understanding not only of the particular societies in the study of which they were reached but for the understanding of any society, including our own.

VI

APPLIED ANTHROPOLOGY

In my earlier lectures I tried to give you a general idea of what social anthropology is in terms of university teaching, of its development as a special department of knowledge, and of the manner and problems of its research. In this final lecture I shall discuss the question most anthropologists must have been asked from time to time. What is the purpose of studying social anthropology?

This question can be variously interpreted and answered. It might be interpreted as an inquiry about the motives that make a man take up social anthropology as a profession. Each anthropologist would probably here give different answers from those of his colleagues. For many of us, including myself, the answer would be either 'I don't quite know' or, in the words of an American colleague, 'I guess I just like going places.'

However, the question generally has the different sense of: What is the use of knowledge about primitive societies? An answer to the question in this form has to be divided into a discussion about its use for the primitive peoples themselves and for those who are responsible for their welfare, and a discussion about its value to the men who study it—to ourselves.

Since social anthropologists mostly study primitive societies, the information they collect and the conclusions they come to obviously have some bearing on problems of the administration and education of primitive peoples. It will at once be acknowledged that if it is the policy of a colonial government to administer a people through their chiefs it is useful to know who are the chiefs and what are their functions and authority and privileges and obligations. Also, if it is intended to administer a people according to their own laws and customs one has first to discover what these are. It is evident also that if it is intended to change a people's economy, for example to alter their system of land tenure, to encourage them to grow export crops, or to institute markets and a money economy, it is of some advantage to be able to estimate, at any rate roughly, what social effects these changes are likely to bring about. If, for example, the system of land tenure is changed there may be repercussions on the people's family and kinship life and on their religion, because family and kinship ties and religious beliefs and cults may be closely bound up with their traditional system of tenure. It is evident also that if a missionary wishes to convert a native people to Christianity some knowledge of their own religious beliefs and practices is required. Otherwise apostolic teaching is impossible, because it has to be through the native language, that is, through the religious concepts of the natives.

The value of social anthropology to administration has been generally recognized from the beginning of the century and both the Colonial Office and colonial governments have shown an increasing interest in anthropological teaching and research. For a good number of years past colonial cadets, before taking up their appointments, have received, among other courses of instruction, instruction in social anthropology at Oxford and Cambridge, and more recently in London. Since the last war colonial officials have been brought home for refresher courses at these three universities and some of them choose social anthropology for special study as an optional subject. In addition, administrative officers have often taken the Anthropological Tripos at Cambridge and occasionally the Diploma or a postgraduate degree in Anthropology at Oxford, and a great many have kept in touch with anthropological developments through membership of the Royal Anthropological Institute.

Colonial governments recognized that while a general and elementary knowledge of anthropology is of value to their officers it is not in itself sufficient to enable them to carry out research, even if they had, as they have not, time and opportunity to conduct it; but the governments have occasionally seconded officers in their service, who have received some further training in anthropology and have shown an aptitude for research, to make studies of peoples in their territories. Some important studies have been made in this way, the most remarkable being the research embodied in the series of volumes by Rattray on the Ashanti of the Gold Coast. Valuable work of the same kind was also done by Dr. Meek in Nigeria and by F. E. Williams and E. W. Pearson Chinnery in New Guinea. It must be said, however, that even at their best the writings of these administrator-anthropologists seldom satisfy the professional scholar. It may perhaps be assumed that they are also not entirely satisfactory from the administrative point of view, because, except in Tanganyika Territory, this mode of conducting research has, I believe, been abandoned by colonial governments.

The government of the Anglo-Egyptian Sudan has always preferred, I think wisely, to finance expeditions by professional anthropologists to carry out special pieces of research or to employ them on short-term contracts for the same purpose, and with intervals research has been going on in that country, successively by Professor and Mrs. Seligman, myself, Dr. Nadel, and Mr. Lienhardt from 1909 to the present time. This method has the advantage that while the anthropologist is gaining experience which will later enable him to take a university post the government is getting its inquiries

SOCIAL ANTHROPOLOGY

made by a fully trained man acquainted with the most recent developments in the subject.

Since the last war the Colonial Office has shown greater interest in social anthropology. It has organized and financed anthropological research in a good number of the colonial territories. This means of getting research done has not been, in my assessment of the results, entirely successful. I strongly support the opinion of those who hold that research is best carried out through university departments, which are then made responsible for the selection and training of the student, for supervision of his research, and for the writing-up and publication of its results. The present policy of the Colonial Office is to organize research through local research institutes. One of these, the Rhodes-Livingstone Institute in Northern Rhodesia, has been operating since 1938, and three new institutes for social research have recently been founded, one at Makerere in Uganda, a second at Ibadan in Nigeria, and a third at Kingston in Jamaica. I think myself that this will not prove to be a substitute for the organization of research through university departments, though local institutes can have a useful function as local centres from which research by students of the universities can be carried out—a role like that of the British Institutes at Rome, Athens, and Ankara.

This has been appreciated elsewhere. An extremely important development for anthropologists has been the creation of Treasury Studentships for research into the languages and cultures of the Far East, the Near East, Eastern Europe, and Africa. Experience during the last war showed that there was a lamentable ignorance about these parts of the world, and a Royal Commission under the chairmanship of the Earl of Scarbrough concluded that this state of affairs could only finally be changed by the building up of a tradition of scholarship in the languages and cultures with which it was concerned.

The admirable plan they proposed included the strengthening of university departments and the creation of new university departments, the provision of studentships for research from the universities by men who would eventually take up teaching posts in them, and the foundation of institutes as local research centres in the parts of the world where these researches would be carried out. In this way it is ensured not only that research is conducted but also that a tradition of scholarship is built up and maintained.

These Treasury Studentships have enabled social anthropologists to carry out in various regions research which might otherwise have been beyond their means; for anthropological research in distant parts is very expensive, and the various endowments which generously help us—such as the Emslie Horniman Anthropological Scholarship Fund, the Goldsmiths Company's Postgraduate Travelling Scholarships, the Leverhulme Grants Committee, and the Viking Fund—cannot cover more than a very small portion of the research urgently required.

Missionary bodies in this country have not shown that they consider some acquaintance with anthropology a useful adjunct to the training of those who are to serve in the missions among primitive peoples. This is partly due to the poverty of the missions, which cannot afford to send their volunteers to the universities where anthropology is taught. It is also partly due, I think, to the suspicion with which anthropology has been regarded in missionary circles. The suspicion has not perhaps been unfounded, for anthropology has always been mixed up with free-thought and has been considered, not unjustly, as anti-religious in tone, and even in aim. Also, missionaries feel, naturally enough, that, as Gabriel Sagard says in his introduction to his book on the Hurons (1632), 'The perfection of men does not consist in seeing much, nor in knowing much, but in carrying out the will and good pleasure of God.' Nevertheless, many individual missionaries have taken a deep interest in anthropology and have realized its value for their own work. Their attitude is well expressed by Pasteur Junod of the Swiss Romande Mission, the author of one of the finest anthropological monographs yet written. He tells us that his aim in collecting the information embodied in this book was partly scientific and partly to help administrative officers and missionaries and to enlighten South African opinion about the natives: 'To work for Science is noble; but to help our fellow men is nobler still.'[1] Another missionary, Dr. Edwin Smith, part-author of an excellent account of the Ba-ila people of Northern Rhodesia, has recently been President of the Royal Anthropological Institute.

In the past it has been chiefly administrators and missionaries who have found that some knowledge of anthropology has helped them to carry out their duties more agreeably and effectively. In the changed situation of today technical experts have become increasingly important in our colonial empire—the doctor, the agricultural officer, the forestry officer, the veterinary officer, the engineer, and so on, and also the trader and representatives of mining and other business interests. At present most of them are expected to carry out their various jobs among peoples about whose way of life and ideas they often know next to nothing.

You will ask how a knowledge of anthropology helps Europeans in their dealings with native peoples. Many anthropologists have for a long time spoken about applied anthropology much as one speaks about applied medicine or engineering. Those who have spoken thus have regarded social anthropology as a natural science which aims at the establishment of laws of social life; and once theoretical generalizations can be established

---

[1] *The Life of a South African Tribe*, 1913, p. 10.

an applied science becomes feasible. We have seen that this normative element in anthropology is, like the concepts of natural law and progress from which it derives, part of its philosophical heritage. As I have earlier said, the eighteenth-century moral philosophers, the nineteenth-century ethnologists, and the majority of the social anthropologists of today have, implicitly or explicitly, taken the natural sciences for their model and assumed that the purpose of anthropology is by prediction and planning to control social change. This assumption is summed up in the phrase 'social engineering'.

It is not surprising therefore that from its earliest years theoretical social anthropology has often been strongly tinged with socialism, especially in France, where both Saint Simon and Comte tried to start positivist religions. It is, I think, clearly the driving impulse behind the work of Durkheim and his colleagues. Their general point of view is well expressed by one of them, Lévy-Bruhl, in an excellent short exposition, *La Morale et la Science des Moeurs* (1903). According to him ethical systems have no effect on conduct whatsoever. They cannot have, because they are merely rationalizations of custom, what is done being right. If a people, for example, kill all twins at birth the practice is moral for that people. Morals are simply rules which actually determine conduct in any society and they therefore vary with variations in the social structure. The moral is what is normal to a given social type at a given phase of development. The task of reason is therefore to mould behaviour by a practical art of ethics derived from a scientific study of social life. This is much the standpoint of almost all writers about social institutions at that period. It was only to have been expected that it should have been shared by many social anthropologists.

Such anthropologists have constantly stressed the

application of their findings to affairs, the emphasis in England being on colonial problems, and in America on political and industrial problems. Its more cautious advocates have, it is true, held that there can only be applied social anthropology when the science of man is much more advanced than it is today; but we find even so cautious and eminent an authority as Professor Radcliffe-Brown writing: 'With the more rapid advance of the pure science itself, and with the co-operation of colonial administrations, we might even look forward to a time when the government and education of native peoples in various parts of the world would make some approach to being an art based on the application of discovered laws of anthropological science.'[1] Less cautious and more popular writers on anthropology, especially in America, have made far-reaching claims for the immediate application of anthropological knowledge in social planning.

If this, what may be called the natural science, view is accepted, it is quite logical to hold further that, since sociological laws are applicable to any society, their main use is rather in the planning of our own society than in controlling the development of primitive societies, which may be regarded as the guinea-pigs of sociological research. After all, it is not only in Africa that there are problems of government, of ownership, of labour migration, of divorce, and so forth. What we discover, for example, about the breakdown of family life among the peoples of our colonial territories can, if a general formula can be derived from the knowledge, be applied to the breakdown of family life in England and America. 'The debt we owe the society that supports us', an American anthropologist, Professor Herskovits, tells

[1] A. R. Radcliffe-Brown, 'Applied Anthropology', *Report of Australian and New Zealand Association for the Advancement of Science*, Section F., 1930, p. 3.

us, 'must be made in terms of long-time payments, in our fundamental contributions towards an understanding of the nature and processes of culture and, through this, to the solution of some of our own basic problems.'[1] What we learn from the yellow and black, as Kipling said in a very different context, will help us a lot with the white.

I have, I hope, made it abundantly and repeatedly clear in these lectures that I do not believe that there can ever be a science of society which resembles the natural sciences. It is not, however, necessary to enter into that question all over again, for I do not think that there is any anthropologist anywhere who would seriously maintain that up to the present time any sociological laws have been discovered; and if there are no laws known, they cannot be applied.

This does not mean that social anthropology cannot be, even in a narrow and technical sense, applied in any way. It only means that it cannot be an applied science like medicine or engineering. Nevertheless, it is a systematic body of knowledge about primitive societies and, like all knowledge of the kind, it can be used to some extent and in a common-sense way in the running of affairs. In the administration and education of backward peoples decisions have to be made, and those responsible for making them are more likely to make wise decisions if they know what the facts are. They are also more likely to avoid serious blunders. Two wars were fought against the Ashanti of the Gold Coast before it was discovered that the Golden Stool of this people, the surrender of which the government had demanded, was believed by the Ashanti to contain the soul of their whole people and could in no circumstances be given up. That anthropological knowledge has been, or can be, of this kind of

[1] Melville J. Herskovits, 'Applied Anthropology and the American Anthropologist', *Science*, 6 March 1936, p. 7.

assistance to administration is evident and has often been stressed by both anthropologists and administrators. It is well summed up in the words written by Professor W. H. Flower in 1884: 'It is absolutely necessary for the statesman who would govern successfully, not to look upon human nature in the abstract and endeavour to apply universal rules, but to consider the special moral, intellectual and social capabilities, wants, and aspirations of each particular race with which he has to deal.'[1]

Obvious though the observation may be, it is I think worth emphasizing that these 'special moral, intellectual and social capabilities, wants, and aspirations' have to be discovered, and also that experience has proved that anthropologists are able to discover them more accurately and quickly than other people. They know what to look for and how to look for it. Time will not allow me to give you more than one example to illustrate how specialist research has been of value to administrations and missions. Among many African peoples one of the ways in which marriage is brought about is by the bridegroom's family and kin handing over cattle to the bride's family and kin. It was for a long time thought that this bridewealth was a purchase and that girls were being sold for cattle. The transaction was therefore condemned by missionaries and forbidden by governments. When it was shown by anthropological research that the transfer of cattle is no more the purchase of a wife than the payment of dowry in western Europe is purchase of a husband, and that the condemnation and abolition of it not only weakened the bonds of marriage and family ties, but also tended to bring about the very degradation of women which they were intended to prevent, a different view began to be taken of it. This is the kind of matter on which laymen might look to anthropology for guidance;

[1] W. H. Flower, The President's Address, *Journal of the Anthropological Institute*, 1884, p. 493.

for the nature and functions of bridewealth can only be discovered by anthropological research.

Besides being in a better position than other people to discover what the facts are, anthropologists are sometimes more likely to estimate correctly the effects of administrative action, because their training accustoms them to look for repercussions where laymen might not look. They may therefore be fairly asked to assist colonial governments, not only by telling them what the facts are, so that policy can be implemented in the light of them, but also by telling them what the effects of any policy are likely to be. It is not an anthropologist's task, however, to suggest what policy should be adopted. Anthropologists may, by their discovery of the facts, influence the means employed in attaining ends of policy and the outlook of those responsible for shaping it, but the knowledge about primitive societies they collect and publish cannot determine what policy is to be pursued.

Policy is determined by overriding considerations. It does not require an anthropologist to tell us that doubtless the people of Bikini Island would be happier if their home had not been turned into a testing ground for atomic bombs. It would also be in vain were anthropologists to explain to governments, as indeed they have done, that if head-hunting among communities in islands of the Pacific is prohibited the peoples concerned may deteriorate and die out. The governments would reply that head-hunting must be stopped regardless of consequences because it is repugnant to natural justice, equity and good government. This is, I think, a good example because it illustrates that ends are determined by values which are axiomatic and do not derive from factual knowledge of circumstances. If those who control policy believe in material prosperity, literacy, democratic institutions, or whatever it may be, they feel that they have to give them to the peoples of their colonial empire.

Whether they are doing right or wrong is a question for moral philosophy, not for social anthropology.

To avoid compromising scholarship anthropologists should eschew questions of policy; and I feel that I should say further that even as fact-finders there is in their dependence for support on governments an element of danger for anthropology and a possibility of conflict between the views of anthropologists and those of governments about what constitutes anthropological research. An anthropologist may be particularly interested, let us say, in some problems of primitive religion and therefore wish to devote a great deal of his attention to them, whereas—governments not generally being interested in such matters—the administration may want chief attention given to problems of labour migration. Or a government may want research done solely into a people's system of land tenure, whereas the anthropologist takes the view that you cannot understand their system of land tenure without a study of their entire social life. Naturally enough, the anthropologist is interested in problems of anthropology, whether these have any practical significance or not. Equally naturally, a colonial government is interested in practical problems, whether they have any theoretical significance or not. Difficulties have arisen on this account. I think myself that the only ultimate solution is for colonial governments to have anthropological posts on their establishments, as they have posts for educationalists, geologists, botanists, parasitologists, and other experts. Some anthropologists will then choose an academic career and others a career in the service of administrations.

I have myself done a considerable amount of research for the government of the Anglo-Egyptian Sudan. As the view of this government about social anthropology corresponds, if I have understood it rightly, with my own, a statement of it will enable me to give you my own opinion about the value of social anthropology to administration. The Sudan Government has, as I have mentioned earlier, for a long time and very generously supported anthropological research. In doing so it has allowed anthropologists to study pretty well where, what, and how they liked. They have chosen the man and let him choose the plan. I think that they have been wise enough to do this because they have never been under the illusion that anything the anthropologist discovered was likely to have any great practical importance. They felt rather that a government ought to some extent to encourage scholarship, and they believed—and this is the point I want to stress—that a knowledge of the languages, cultures, and social life of the peoples of the Sudan has an immense value for administrative officials and others, quite apart from whether it solves any immediate practical problems or not.

One can, I think, look at the matter in this way. If a man were to take a diplomatic or business appointment in France, life would be much more agreeable for him, not to speak of the French, and he would make a much better diplomat or business man, were he to learn the French language and to know a good deal about French social life and the working of their institutions. It is the same with a man living among a primitive people. If he knows what they are saying and what they are doing, and their ideas and values, he will not only have a much deeper understanding of the people but will also probably administer them more justly and effectively.

A seventeenth-century traveller, de la Crequinière, whom I have quoted in an earlier lecture, expresses this point of view succinctly. After giving advice to travellers, based on his experience of the East Indians, to keep an inquiring mind but to remain steadfast in their own religion, to tolerate and try to understand strange

customs and to behave well in foreign lands, to avoid
falling in love, which is distracting, to avoid gambling
and confidence tricksters, and to study history, languages
and geography, he concludes: 'He who knows how to
travel as he should, will reap great advantages: he will
improve his mind by his remarks, govern his heart by
his reflections, and refine his carriage by conversing with
honourable persons of many countries; and after this,
he will be much better qualified to live genteelly, for he
will know how to accommodate himself to the customs
of different people, and so in all probability to the different humours of those he is obliged to visit: by this means
he will never do anything to others, which he knows to
be contrary to their inclination; which is almost the only
point wherein consists what we now call, the Art of
Living.'[1]

I do not believe that anthropological knowledge can
be applied to any extent in the arts of administration and
education among primitive peoples in any other than in
this very general cultural sense—in the influence it has
in shaping the attitude of the European towards native
peoples. The understanding of a people's way of life
generally arouses sympathy for them, and sometimes
deep devotion to their service and interests. The native,
as well as the European, is then benefited.

I will briefly mention one further particular use social
anthropology may have for the peoples whose life is
investigated and described. We would ourselves have
been richer, and deeply grateful, had some Roman
anthropologist bequeathed to us an exact and detailed
description of the social life of our Celtic and Anglo-
Saxon ancestors. One day native peoples all over the
world may be glad to have just such a record of the life
of their forbears written by impartial students whose

[1] *Customs of the East Indians*, 1705, p. 159. (Translated from *Conformité des Coutumes des Indiens Orientaux*, 1704, pp. 251–2.)

ambition is to give as full and as true an account as they can.

Social anthropology may occasionally resolve problems of administration. It makes for a sympathetic understanding of other peoples. It also provides valuable material for the historian of the future. But I do not myself attach as much importance to any service it is or may be in these respects as to the general attitudes, or habits of mind, it forms in us by what it teaches us about the nature of social life. It accustoms us to viewing any social activity in any society in the context of the whole social life of which it is part; and also, to see always the particular in the light of the more general.

The social anthropologist aims at revealing the structural forms or patterns which lie behind the complexity and apparent confusion of actualities in the society he is studying; and he does this by seeking to make abstractions from social behaviour and to relate these to one another in such a way that the social life can be perceived as a set of interconnected parts, as a whole. This can, of course, only be done by analysis; but the analysis is made, not as an end—to resolve social life into isolated elements—but as a means—to bring out its essential unity by the subsequent integration of the abstractions reached by analysis. This is why I have stressed that for me social anthropology, whatever else it may be, is an art.

The social anthropologist aims also at showing, by comparing one society with another, the common features of institutions as well as their particularities in each society. He seeks to show how some characteristics of an institution or set of ideas are peculiar to a given society, how others are common to all societies of a certain type, and how yet others are found in all human societies—are universals. The characteristics he looks for are of a functional order, so that he is here again, but on a higher level of abstraction, looking for a dynamic order in social life, patterns which are common to all societies of the same general type and patterns which are universal. Whether he is attempting to reach conclusions about one society or about many or all societies, his procedure is the same: to reach, by analysis, abstractions from complex social actualities, and then to relate these abstractions to one another in such a way that total social relations can be presented as a design, and so perceived by the mind in perspective and as an interconnected whole, with their significant features brought into relief. He is to be judged by whether he succeeds in doing this, and not by whether what he writes is immediately useful.

It is in the light of this conception of the aims of social anthropology that I would ask you to consider its significance for us as persons and its value as a small part of the knowledge of our culture. Since I have this conception of its aims, you will understand why I have emphasized in these lectures that a study of primitive societies is worth pursuing for its own sake, whether or not it can be put to any practical or scientific purpose. I am sure that none of you would hold that a knowledge of ancient Athens, of medieval France, or of renaissance Italy is valueless merely because it does not help us very much in a practical way to solve problems of our own society at the present time, or because it does not aid us in formulating sociological laws. I need not therefore try to convince you that knowledge which cannot be put to any immediate practical purpose, or cannot be reduced to scientific formulae, may yet have great importance both for individuals in their own lives and for our whole society.

Some of you may be thinking, however, and one sometimes hears it said, that it is all very well reading about ancient Athens, medieval France, and renaissance Italy, but who wants to read about a lot of savages? Those who ask this question call us barbarologists. I find this view hard to understand, and it has certainly not been that taken by inquiring minds ever since knowledge of stranger peoples, and in particular of primitive peoples, began to filter into the thought of western Europe. I have remarked in earlier lectures how from the sixteenth century onwards educated men were interested in the reports of travellers about savage peoples, in the remarkable similarities of thought and behaviour no less than in the wide divergences of culture they revealed; and how philosophers were particularly engaged by those reports which described primitive institutions. I fancy that they were more interested in the institutions of the Caribs and the Iroquois than in those of medieval England.

Their curiosity is easy to understand, for primitive peoples must have an interest for anyone who reflects at all on the nature of man and society. Here are men without revealed religion, without a written language, without any developed scientific knowledge, often entirely naked and having only the crudest tools and habitations—men in the raw, as it were—who yet live, and for the most part live happily, in communities of their kind. We cannot imagine ourselves living, far less living contentedly, in such conditions, and we wonder— and I think we *should* wonder—what it is which enables them to live together in harmony, and to face courageously the hazards of life with so little to aid them in their battle against nature and fate. The mere fact that savages have no motor cars, do not read newspapers, do not buy and sell, and so on, far from making them less, makes them more, interesting; for here man confronts destiny in all its harshness and pain without the cushioning of civilization, its anodynes and consolations. No wonder the philosophers thought that such men must live in constant fear and misery.

That they do not do so is because they live in a moral

order which gives them security and values which make life bearable. For closer inspection shows that beneath this superficial simplicity of life there lie complex social structures and rich cultures. We are so used to thinking of culture and social institutions in terms of material civilization and size, that we miss them altogether among primitive peoples unless we search for them. We then discover that all primitive peoples have a religious faith, expressed in dogmas and rites; that they have marriage, brought about by ceremonial and other observances, and family life centred in a home; that they have a kinship system, often a very complicated system and wider than anything of the kind in our own society; that they have clubs and associations for special purposes; that they have rules, often elaborate rules, of etiquette and manners; that they have regulations, often enforced by courts, constituting codes of civil and criminal law; that their languages are often extremely complex, phonetically and grammatically, and have vast vocabularies; that they have a vernacular literature of poetry, rich in symbolism, and of chronicles, myths, folk tales, and proverbs; that they have plastic arts; that they have systems of husbandry which require considerable knowledge of seasons and soils and of plant and animal life; that they are expert fishers and hunters and adventurers by sea and land; and that they have great stores of knowledge—of magic, of witchcraft, and of oracles and divination—to which we are strangers.

It is surely a prejudice and a fashion to hold that these cultures and societies are not as much worth knowing about as others, that an educated man should know about ancient Egypt, Greece, and Rome but need know nothing about Maoris, Eskimoes, or Bantu. This is surely the same mentality as that which centred in post-renaissance and post-reformation time for so long turned its back on the Middle Ages, and centred in space in the Mediterranean and northern Europe treated the history, literature, art, and philosophy of India as of no account. This ethnocentric attitude has to be abandoned if we are to appreciate the rich variety of human culture and social life. The sculptures of West Africa must not be evaluated by the canons of Greek sculpture. The languages of Melanesia must not be treated as failures to conform to the rules of Latin grammar. Magical beliefs and practices are not in the least understood by measuring them by the rules of western science. The hordes of the Australian aborigines are not to be judged against Birmingham and Manchester. Each people has confronted in its own way the problems that arise when men live together and try to preserve their values and hand them down to their children, and its solutions are as worthy of our attention as those of any other people. A primitive society may be small, but is a beetle or a butterfly less interesting than an ox?

This brings me to a more general aspect of social anthropology, what it teaches us, not about primitive societies as such, but about the nature of human society in general. What we learn about one society can tell us something about another and therefore about all societies, whether historical or of our own time.

Let me take some limited and historical examples. Much has been written about the pre-Islamic Bedouin of Arabia, but there are many questions about their social structure which are difficult to answer from the historical evidences. One way of shedding light on these problems is to study the social structure of the Bedouin Arabs of today, who in most respects lead the same kind of life as those of ancient times. Much has been written about the feud in early periods of English history, but here again we are greatly helped towards solving many problems concerning it by a study of how feuds work in barbarous societies of the present day. It is difficult for us now to understand witch trials which took place in, let us say, seventeenth-century England. We can learn a lot about them by a study of witchcraft in central African societies, where people still believe in witches and hold them responsible for damage to their neighbours. One has, of course, to act with great caution in seeking from a study of social phenomena in one society interpretative guidance in the study of similar phenomena in another society; but in fact, however much in some respects the phenomena may differ, in other and basic respects they are alike.

What I am saying is fairly obvious. In every society, however simple, we find some kind of family life, recognition of ties of kinship, an economy, a political system, social status, religious cult, ways of settling disputes and of punishing crime, organized recreation, and so forth, together with a material culture, and a body of knowledge of nature, of techniques, and of tradition. If we want to understand the common features of any kind of institution in human societies in general, and also to understand the different forms it takes and the different roles it plays in different societies, we are clearly aided by a study of the simpler societies as well as of the more complex. What we discover in the study of a primitive society about the nature of one of its institutions makes this institution more intelligible to us in any society, including our own. If we are attempting to understand Islam, for instance, or Christianity or Hinduism, it is a great help towards our understanding of it if we know that certain features of it are universals, features of all religions, including those of the most primitive peoples; that others are features of certain types of religion, and yet others are distinctive of that religion alone.

Fundamentally, I would put the case for social anthropology in this way. It enables us, from one angle, to see mankind as a whole. When we get accustomed to the anthropological way of looking at human cultures and societies we move easily from the particular to the general and back again. If we talk of the family, we do not mean just the family of western Europe of today, but a universal institution, of which the family of western Europe is only one special form with many distinctive peculiarities. When we think of religion we do not think only of Christianity but of the vast number of cults which are practised, and have been practised, throughout the world. Only by understanding other cultures and societies does one see one's own in perspective, and come to understand it better against a background of the totality of human experience and endeavour. If I may revert to my last lecture—Dr. Margaret Mead gained some understanding in Samoa of American problems of adolescence; Malinowski shed light on problems of incentives in British industry by his study of Trobriand exchange of ritual objects, and I think that I gained some understanding of communist Russia by studying witchcraft among the Azande. To sum it all up, I believe that social anthropology helps us to understand better, and in whatever place or time we meet him, that wondrous creature man.

SELECT BIBLIOGRAPHY

GENERAL

Bryson, Gladys, *Man and Society*, Princeton, 1945.

Firth, Raymond, *Human Types*, London, 1938.

Forde, C. D., *Habitat, Economy and Society*, London, 1934.

Haddon, A. C., *History of Anthropology*, London, 1934.

Hodgen, M. T., *The Doctrine of Survivals*, London, 1936.

Kroeber, A. L., *Anthropology*, New York, 1923 (new edit. 1948).

Lowie, R. H., *The History of Ethnological Theory*, London, 1937.

Notes and Queries in Anthropology, London, 1874 (6th edit. to appear in 1951).

Penniman, T. K., *A Hundred Years of Anthropology*, London, 1935.

Radin, Paul, *The Method and Theory of Ethnology*, New York and London, 1933.

THEORETICAL WORKS

Eighteenth Century

Dunbar, James, *Essays on the History of Mankind in Rude and Cultivated Ages*, London, 1780.

Ferguson, Adam, *An Essay on the History of Civil Society*, Edinburgh, 1767.

Hume, David, *A Treatise of Human Nature*, London, 1739–40.

Kames, Lord, *Historical Law-Tracts*, Edinburgh, 1758.

Monboddo, Lord, *Of the Origin and Progress of Language*, Edinburgh, 1773–92.

Montesquieu, Baron de, *De L'Esprit des Lois*, Geneva, 1748. (English trans., *The Spirit of the Laws*, by T. Nugent, New York, 1949).

Saint Simon, Comte de, *Oeuvres de Saint Simon et d'Enfantin*, Paris, 1865.

Nineteenth Century

Bachofen, J. J., *Das Mutterrecht*, Stuttgart, 1861.

Bastian, Adolf, *Der Mensch in der Geschichte*. Leipzig, 1860.

Comte, Auguste, *Cours de Philosophie Positive*, Paris, 1830 onwards.

Coulanges, Fustel de, *La Cité Antique*, Paris, 1864 (English trans., *The Ancient City*, by William Small, Boston and New York, 1882.)

Durkheim, Emile, *De la Division du Travail Social*, Paris, 1893 (English trans., *The Division of Labour in Society*, by George Simpson, New

131

York, 1933.); *Les Règles de la Méthode Sociologique*, Paris, 1895 (English trans., *The Rules of Sociological Method*, by Sarah A. Solway and John H. Mueller., Glencoe (Illinois), 1938.

Frazer, Sir James, *The Golden Bough*, London, 1890.

Hubert, H., and Mauss, M., 'Essai sur la Nature et la Fonction du Sacrifice', *L'Année Sociologique*, T. 11, Paris, 1897-98.

Maine, Sir Henry, *Ancient Law*, London, 1861; *Village-Communities in the East and West*, London, 1871.

McLennan, J. F., *Primitive Marriage*, London, 1865; *Studies in Ancient History*, London, 1886 and 1896.

Morgan, Lewis H., *Systems of Consanguinity and Affinity of the Human Family*, Washington, 1871.; *Ancient Society*, London, 1877.

Smith, W. Robertson, *Kinship and Marriage in Early Arabia*, London, 1885; *Lectures on the Religion of the Semites*, London, 1889.

Spencer, Herbert, *The Study of Sociology*, London, 1872 onwards; *The Principles of Sociology*, New York, 1882-83.

Steinmetz, S. R., *Ethnologische Studien zur ersten Entwicklung der Strafe*, Leiden and Leipsig, 1894.

Tylor, Sir Edward, *Researches into the Early History of Mankind*, London, 1865.; *Primitive Culture*, London, 1871.

Westermarck, Edward, *The History of Human Marriage*, London, 1891.

Twentieth Century

Benedict, Ruth, *Patterns of Culture*, Boston and New York, 1934.

Cassirer, Ernst, *An Essay on Man*, New Haven, 1944.

Collingwood, R. G., *The Idea of History*, Oxford, 1946.

Durkheim, Emile, *Les Formes Elémentaires de la Vie Religieuse*, Paris, 1912 (Engl. trans., *The Elementary Forms of the Religious Life*, by J. W. Swain, London, 1915.)

Ginsberg, M., *Reason and Unreason in Society*, London, 1947.

Grönbech, V., *The Culture of the Teutons*, 2 vols., Copenhagen and London, 1931. (Trans. from the Danish ed. of 1909-12.)

Hobhouse, L. T., *Morals in Evolution*, London, 1906.

Hubert, H. and Mauss, M., 'Esquisse d'une Théorie générale de la Magie', *L'Année Sociologique*, T.VII, Paris, 1902-3.

Lévy-Bruhl, L., *Les Fonctions Mentales dans les Sociétés Inférieures*, Paris, 1912 (English trans., *How Natives Think*, by Lilian A. Clare London, 1926); *La Mentalité Primitive*, Paris, 1922 (English trans. *Primitive Mentality*, by Lilian A. Clare, London, 1923.)

Lévi-Strauss, C., *Les Structures Elémentaires de la Parenté*, Paris, 1949.

Lowie, R. H., *Primitive Society*, London, 1920.

SELECT BIBLIOGRAPHY

MacIver, R. M., *Society*, London, 1937.

Malinowski, B., *Magic, Science, and Religion and other Essays*, Glencoe (Illinois), 1948.

Marett, R. R., *The Threshold of Religion*, London, 1909.

Mauss, M., 'Essai sur le Don', *L'Année Sociologique*, N. S. 1, Paris, 1923–4.

Nieboer, H. J., *Slavery as an Industrial System*, The Hague, 1900.

Radcliffe-Brown, A. R., *The Social Organization of Australian Tribes* (*Oceania Monographs*, No. I,) Melbourne, 1931; *Structure and Function in Primitive Society—Essays and Addresses*, London, *In the press*.

Rivers, W. H. R., *Kinship and Social Organization*, London, 1914; *Social Organization*, London, 1926.

Simmel, Georg, *Soziologie*, Leipzig, 1908.

Tawney, R. H., *Religion and the Rise of Capitalism*, London, 1926.

Teggart, F. J., *Theory of History*, New Haven, 1925.

Van Gennep, A., *Les Rites de Passage*, Paris, 1909.

Vinogradoff, Sir Paul, *English Society in the Eleventh Century*, Oxford, 1908; *Outlines of Historical Jurisprudence*, Oxford, 1920.

Weber, Max, *Wirtschaft und Gesellschaft*, 1921–23. (English trans., *The Theory of Social and Economic Organization*, by A. R. Henderson and Talcott Parsons, London, 1947.)

Wiese, Leopold von, *Allgemeine Soziologie*, Munich and Leipzig, 1924.

FIELDWORK MONOGRAPHS

Arensberg, Conrad M., and Kimball, Solon T., *Family and Community in Ireland*, Cambridge, Mass., 1940.

Brown, A. R., *The Andaman Islanders*, Cambridge, 1922.

Drake, St. Clair and Cayton, Horace R., *Black Metropolis*, New York, 1945.

Evans-Pritchard, E. E., *Witchcraft, Oracles and Magic among the Azande*, Oxford, 1937; *The Nuer*, Oxford, 1940.

Firth, Raymond, *We, the Tikopia*, London, 1936.

Fortes, M., *The Dynamics of Clanship among the Tallensi*, Oxford, 1945; *The Web of Kinship among the Tallensi*, Oxford, 1949.

Fortes, M. and Evans-Pritchard, E. E., (editors), *African Political Systems*, Oxford, 1940.

Fortune, R. F., *Sorcerers of Dobu*, London, 1932.

Hunter, Monica, *Reaction to Conquest*, London, 1936.

Junod, H. A., *The Life of a South African Tribe*, 2 vols., Neuchatel and London, 1912–13.

Kuper, Hilda, *An African Aristocracy: Rank among the Swazi*, Oxford, 1947.

Lafitau, Joseph François, *Moeurs des Sauvages Ameriquains*, Paris, 1724.

Malinowski, B., *Argonauts of the Western Pacific*, London, 1922; *Crime and Custom in Savage Society*, London, 1926; *Coral Gardens and their Magic*, London, 1935.

Mead, Margaret, *Coming of Age in Samoa*, London, 1929; *Growing up in New Guinea*, London, 1931.

Nadel, S. F., *A Black Byzantium*, Oxford, 1942.

Peristiany, J. G., *The Social Institutions of the Kipsigis*, 1939.

Rattray, R. S., *Ashanti Law and Constitution*, Oxford, 1929.

Redfield, Robert, *The Folk Culture of Yucatan*, 1941.

Rivers, W. H. R., *The Todas*, London, 1906,

Schapera, I., *A Handbook of Tswana Law and Custom*, Oxford, 1938; *Married Life in an African Tribe*, Oxford, 1940.

Seligman, C. G. and B. Z., *The Veddas*, Cambridge, 1911.

Smith, E. W., and Dale, A. M., *The Ila-Speaking Peoples of Northern Rhodesia*, London, 1920.

Spencer, Sir Baldwin and Gillen, F. J., *The Arunta*, 2 vols., London, 1927.

Made in the USA
Coppell, TX
27 February 2022

74164422R00083